Money Making Madne$$

Also by Lynn A. Dralle:

The Unofficial Guide to Making Money on eBay
John Wiley & Sons, Inc., 2006

How to Sell Antiques and Collectibles on eBay...
and Make a Fortune!
with Dennis Prince; McGraw Hill, 2005

The 100 Best Things I've Sold on eBay
2004

i sell on eBay Tracking Binder
1999

i buy on eBay Tracking Binder
1999

The Unauthorized Beanie Baby Guide
with Lee Dralle; Scholastic, 1998

The Book of Beanie Babies
with Lee Dralle; AKA, 1998

More 100 Best Things
I've Sold on eBay

Money
Making
Madne$$

My Story Continues
by The Queen of Auctions
Lynn A. Dralle

"It's Still Fun!"

All Aboard, Inc.

Preface

When I wrote *The 100 Best Things I've Sold on eBay,* my editor thought that we should use the preface to explain that it was not intended as a how-to book. It turns out that we were wrong. Not only did *The 100 Best Things I've Sold on eBay* teach readers how to sell on eBay, but they were inspired and entertained by it. The book turned out to be a gentle introduction for the inquisitive into the world of eBay. Aren't we all a little bit curious? I have been overwhelmed with letters and emails telling me that *The 100 Best* got them out of their comfort zones (and easy chairs) and into the world of selling on eBay. I want to take this opportunity to thank all the readers of *The 100 Best* who sent me these amazing letters and emails. You have made my day, every single day of the year, with your kindness.

Since 1998, I've made a career out of eBay. In addition to buying and selling as a PowerSeller on eBay, I've taught classes on how to run an eBay business, created an auction tracking system for eBayers (*i buy* and *i sell,* carried in the eBay on-line store), written numerous books about eBay, and produced a DVD, "Trash to Cash," about making money through online auctions.

Money Making Madness is a collection of stories about some of the most memorable auctions I've been involved with on eBay. It contains some great tips and lessons for selling on eBay, but it is also about my friends, my family, my grandmother and me. Why is my grandmother such a big part of this book? There are lots of reasons. She's the one who got me started in the antiques and collectibles business, and she taught me most of what I know about antiques. For me, every story about eBay is also in some sense a story about my grandmother.

Money Making Madness is the second book in *The 100 Best Things I've Sold on eBay series.* The stories and items in this collection are different, but a lot of the messages are the same. All the great lessons that I learned from my grandmother can still be found tucked inside these pages. Things like, "Believe in yourself," "Never give up," and "Help others" are some of my grandmother's wonderful snippets of advice. My grandmother passed away in the year 2000, and I still miss her every day. Writing this second installment gave me the opportunity to spend some time with her again. For that, I thank you.

Now that you have an idea of what this book is all about, I hope you enjoy reading it as much as I enjoyed writing it!

© Copyright 2006 by L.A. Dralle

First Edition 2006

ISBN: 978-0-9768393-0-9

For more information write:

All Aboard, Inc.
P.O. Box 14103
Palm Desert, CA 92255

AllAboard@mail.com
www.TheQueenofAuctions.com

Designed by: Lee Dralle, Becky Raney and Lynn A. Dralle
Edited by: Susan Thornberg

Printed in the United States of America
Print & Copy Factory
4055 Irongate Road
Bellingham, WA 98226
www.printcopyfactory.com

This book is dedicated to
Peter J. Gineris

Thank you for your unwavering support, belief and encouragement.

Acknowledgments

My greatest thanks to:
Cheryl Leaf
Lee Dralle
Susan Thornberg
Becky and Larry Raney
Houston and Indiana
Sharon Chase
Wayne and Sue Dralle
Kristin Dralle
Melanie Souve
Peter Gineris
Maureen Arcand
Maria Cota
eBay
My book, ezine and blog readers
Podcast listeners
My eBay students
AND all our great eBay customers!

Contents

Introduction

More 100 Best Things

Afterword

Introduction

My Grandmother

In November of 1950 in Bellingham, Washington, my grandmother opened her antiques and gift store on the corner of Northwest and Illinois. It would remain open for 52 years. "Cheryl Leaf Antiques and Gifts" was the name of her 200-square-foot shop, and over the years, the building (which also housed her living quarters) would eventually grow to 8,000 square feet. It was filled from floor to rafters with treasures she had purchased abroad, through "wanted" ads, from walk-in customers, from other dealers, and from buying entire estates. My grandmother never went to garage sales. Fast forward to today, where I make my living going to garage sales and selling what I find on eBay.

But let's take a little closer look at the history of Cheryl Leaf. In the 1960's, she started bringing large containers of items over from Europe. Way ahead of the curve—that was my grandmother. In the 1970's, she was big into collector's plates and made a fortune with them. In the 1980's, antiques shows were all the rage. She went to between twelve and eighteen a year, and spent a lot of time on the road. In the 1990's, I returned home to Bellingham to run the antiques store after she fell and broke her hip. We remodeled the entire store and got into the Beanie Baby business. That was a boon and a half.

I grew up working for my grandmother. She would take me to antiques shows when I was a little girl, and I worked for her most days after school and on weekends. My grandmother was my best friend and mentor. She was one of those people who always had a twinkle in her eye and loved life. My son said to me this morning, "Thanks for bringing us into the world. I like it here." That sounded so much like my grandmother talking. Every day was an adventure to her. Running the store with my grandmother was not work—it was play. I miss those days, and I miss my grandmother.

eBay

I started buying on eBay in 1998 after we lost our franchise with Ty (the maker of Beanie Babies) and I needed stock to replace those sales. I was intimidated by the thought of selling on eBay and stayed away as long as possible, but my grandmother got sick in 1999 and we had to raise a lot of money quickly for her nursing care expenses. I guess you could say I was forced into selling on eBay. With all of my grandmother's inventory, we were selling $20,000 a month before we knew it. Once I got started selling, I couldn't stop. I was hooked. I don't think I have taken more than four weeks off from selling on eBay since 1999. I still put 100 new items on each week.

When my grandmother passed away in 2000, I took another two years to liquidate the store, using an estate specialist and eBay. There was just so much stuff. After two years, I finally decided to divide up the eBay-worthy items that remained into four portions for the inheritors: me, my brother Lee, my sister Kristin (Kiki), and my mom Sharon. That way, the very painful liquidation process wouldn't drag on indefinitely. Each inheritor would be responsible for disposing of his or her own items. We finally closed the doors to my grandmother's brick-and-mortar store in 2002. It was a sad day.

The beauty of eBay was that it allowed me to live anywhere. I had moved back to Bellingham in 1993 to run the store, and I was missing Southern California. I realized that I could live anywhere, and in October of 2002, my kids and I moved to Palm Desert.

▼ WHATCOM BUSINESS NOTES

Family closes grandma's antique shop in Bellingham

RETAIL: 51-year-old Cheryl Leaf Antiques will continue to operate online.

Cheryl Leaf's Antiques & Gifts will close Friday after nearly 52 years of business at 2828 Northwest Ave.

During the shop's final hours, 10:30 a.m. to 6 p.m. today and Friday, most items will be marked 70 percent off. Newer gift items will be marked down 30 percent, with some exceptions.

Cheryl Leaf opened her antiques and gift store in November of 1950 and operated it on her own until about 10 years ago, when her granddaughter Lynn Dralle moved here from Los Angeles and helped her manage the business. Leaf died Aug. 2, 2000, and Lynn and her brother, Lee Dralle of Los Angeles, and sister, Kristin Dralle of Bellingham, and their mother, Sharon Chase of Bellingham, inherited her legacy. They decided to close the store on the

PHILIP A. DWYER

anniversary of Leaf's death. "It's really not the same without my grandma," Lynn said of the shop. "It was her passion. She would get up at

FAMILY BUSINESS: Cheryl Leaf Antiques owners (from left) — sisters Kristin Dralle, Lynn Dralle and mother Sharon Chase — are closing their 51-year-old store Friday. The store was started in 1950 by grandmother Cheryl Leaf, who died in 2000.

5 a.m. in the morning and work until about 2 a.m. It was so fortunate that she did what she loved. She worked right up until she

died at age 88."

Leaf traveled around the world, buying antiques in Europe in the 1960s before it became fashionable. She also strung beads, made jewelry and collected lamp parts and created her own lamp designs from them. Lynn Dralle said there are many items still remaining in the attic and long-time customers are now getting the chance to buy items that Leaf kept in her basement.

"It's a trip to come in here and see what this one woman did," Dralle said. "She really was amazing."

She decided last year not to buy the business from her family.

"I thought about buying it but retail has changed so drastically in the last several years with Internet and eBay," she said.

Although the store will close and the building will be sold, Lynn Dralle said she would continue to sell antiques and collectibles online through eBay and at antiquesandgifts.com. Cus-

tomer sign-up and a free newsletter are available at queenofauctions.com. Dralle said she will stick to collectibles such as Danish Christmas Plates, Yankee Candles and Groovy Girls.
— *Linda Partlow*

The 100 Best Things I've Sold on eBay

About six months after arriving in California, I decided I wanted to write a book honoring my grandmother. I had started writing it focusing on the hundred most important things I had learned from her, but it was slow going. In September of 2003, I was teaching a class about eBay for The Learning Annex in Los Angeles. I told a story about an Edwardian mourning case (See #74 in *The 100 Best Things I've Sold on eBay*) that I'd sold earlier in the year. One of the women in the class yelled out, "That story gave me goosebumps!" My stories were her favorite part of the entire three-hour class. Wow! I realized that I had lots of stories to tell about my eBay successes (and failures).

After hearing my student's "goosebumps" comment, I realized that I could combine my eBay stories and my grandmother's lessons into a single book. I could use my eBay experiences as a framework for my grandmother's story—the lessons she taught me, the stories she told, the life she lived. I was excited! When I started writing that book, I couldn't stop! That book is *The 100 Best Things I've Sold on eBay,* and it is the first in this series. Every day I get an email from someone that has read *The 100 Best,* and they tell me what an inspiration it has been to them. That warms my heart.

More 100 Best Things I've Sold on eBay—Money Making Madness

I have been buying and selling on eBay for a long time now. What a learning experience it has been! When I first started, eBay wasn't as user-friendly as it is now. I also found that I had to re-learn everything that I had been taught in the antiques store. Things that would sell in our shop in Bellingham, WA, might not bring as much on eBay, or even be desirable at all. On the flip side, things that I wouldn't ever consider stocking in our store sold for big bucks on eBay—things like empty vintage cereal boxes, skateboards and insulators. *The 100 Best* books give me the opportunity to share many of the lessons I've learned with readers in a fun and entertaining format.

This book has more items that I actually had to go out and buy than the previous *100 Best* book. That is one reason this edition is so fun. I was scared at first to leave the shop and see if I could really make a living by going to garage sales—which is the complete opposite of how my grandmother got her stock. I am happy to report that it is working out incredibly well for me. In fact, the items that I have sold on eBay for the most money are not things I inherited, but things I bought at garage and estate sales for $2 to $20. See #11 (Walt Disney Art) and #68 (AE Crowell Song Bird).

I waited two years to write this edition, so that I would have another wonderful 100 items to talk about. It was a long time, and I was itching to get going again so that I could revisit all the memories I had of my time with my grandmother, Cheryl Leaf. The time finally came for me to write this book and I was thrilled. I couldn't wait to get started. My best friend from high school, Melanie Souve, came up with the title and I love it. Welcome to *Money Making Madness!*

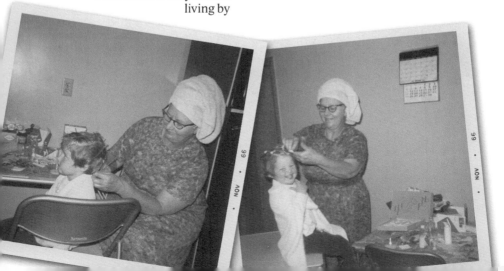

Money Making Madne$$

#1 White Heart Beads

$0.00
Paid
From: Inheritance

Hudson's Bay White Heart Trade Beads-1700s-WOW

Description:

Very early 15" strand of white heart or core beads. This strand dates to the 1700's to 1800's. It is mostly red with white interiors. The beads are about ⅛" by ³⁄₁₆". These are beautiful red white heart trade beads and were handmade in Italy. The only way to make these beads this beautiful red color was to add a small amount of gold to the glass batch. Used by the Hudson's Bay Company as the main form of trade with Native Americans for fur pelts.

Winning Bid:

$79.⁰⁰

Ended: 10/19/03
History: 13 bids
Starting Bid: $9.99
Winner: Punta Gorda, FL

Viewed

 X

White Heart Beads #1

The Story

My grandmother was a strange bird. She wouldn't let us throw anything away, ever! She was the consummate recycler, even before people knew what recycling was. When she got junk mail, she reused the envelopes. After she cracked the last egg, she would use the empty carton for sorting beads. When her father's post-Depression company, Sussex Motors, ordered new invoices and threw out the old, she would grab them for notepaper. And so on.

This can all be attributed to her growing up during the Depression. Her father, George Sussex, owned the bank in Cashmere, Washington; the family was very prominent. She was seventeen years old when the stock market crashed. George insisted on paying back each of his depositors out of his own pocket. By the time she was nineteen years old, her father's remarkable integrity had cost the family everything. She had just finished her sophomore year at the State College of Washington (now Washington State University) and had to drop out of school. There just wasn't any money left for a girl to finish college.

Not having a college degree didn't hurt my grandmother one bit in the business world. She was amazing. She never spent her disposable income on herself—oh, no. It always went right back into inventory. My grandmother loved beads and would buy them by the barrelful. She especially loved the Italian beads made in the 1700's and 1800's for trading purposes.

She used her "recycled" notepaper to record how many strands of each type of bead she owned and what she had paid for them. She would tuck these notes into the shoeboxes that stored the beads. Notice that she had 213 strands of white hearts (named for their white centers) for which she paid $15 each. That is over $3,000 worth of beads! Overall, this one little piece of scrap paper listed beads worth $6,880! And this was just one box.

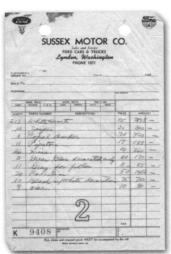

You can imagine how many beads we were left with when she passed away. It was overwhelming.

I found about 50 strands of white hearts in one of my inheritance boxes. I am sure my mom, sister and brother got just as many! I had been putting them on eBay one at a time, but never got more than $20 per strand for them. Then one week when I was doing my "Completed auction" research on eBay, I found some really great information.

It turns out that these beads were used not just for trade with Africa, but also for trade with Native Americans. The Hudson's Bay Company used these as their main source of currency for buying fur pelts. With all of that information in my listing, this strand sold for $79. Now that's more like it!

#2 Hanging Library Lamp

$10.00
Paid

From:
Church rummage sale

OLD Hanging Library Parlor Lamp-Butterfly-WOW

Description:

This is an amazing hanging library or parlor lamp. It is Victorian and I would date it to the 1880's to 1890's. The lamp shade is white with a hand painted floral design featuring a butterfly. Shade is 14" across. It is fantastic because it is all original. The crown and all the brass have the same design and match! Amazing. 42" tall.

Winning Bid: **$425.00**

Ended: 10/20/03
History: 29 bids
Starting Bid: $99
Winner: La Mesa, CA

Viewed

000237 X

Hanging Library Lamp #2

The Story

I had been living in California for almost a year at this point and I had not been going to many garage sales. I was making my living selling things out of the 80 boxes that I had inherited. It was finally time to stop tapping into my grandmother's items and see if I could make a living on my own. Another reason I wanted to stop selling things out of these boxes was because every time I opened one and saw things from the shop, or my grandmother's personal items, or things written in her writing, they brought back so many good memories. I didn't ever want to get to the bottom of those piles.

There was a church rummage sale advertised in the paper and I got there right when they were putting items out. I checked on all the tables and didn't see much, so I decided to take my own advice and have one more look around, paying special attention to the areas under tables. On the ground against the back wall, I spotted a large box with a lampshade peeking out. I investigated further and started shaking with excitement when I realized it was an antique, hand-painted large library shade. When I looked further into the box, I saw the brass frame and glass prisms. I knew all about library hanging lamps from my grandmother. She loved antique lighting and her shop was filled with lamps like this. I was lucky to have learned all about this category from her because it is a very profitable one on eBay.

I didn't want to unpack all the pieces of the lamp and risk other people realizing what it

was, so I carried it over to the checkout table and asked the nice gentleman, Jack (who was doing all the pricing), "How much?" He peaked inside and said, "How about $10?" "That sounds fair," I replied. "I'll take it." I carried it out to my car filled with glee.

I didn't unpack the lamp to check its condition or to see if it was complete at the sale. Why? Because another dealer or worker may have spotted it and tried to drive up the price. Better to leave it packed and take my chances with the pricing. If he had asked $50, I would have unpacked it and checked it all out. For $10, I had nothing to lose.

I got it home and put it all together. It was a beaut. All original and complete except for ten missing prisms. I couldn't wait to get it listed on eBay. I started the auction at $99 with no reserve because that way I would be sure to make ten times my purchase price (that is always my goal), but leave the price low enough to encourage bidding. My strategy paid off, and it sold for $425 with 29 bids. Wow!

#3 Set of Furnivals China

$15.00 Paid

From: Church rummage sale

Furnivals Flow Blue Denmark Soup Tureen RARE

Description:
We were lucky enough to find this fantastic bunch of Furnivals flow blue in the Denmark Pattern. We have multiple auctions up this week with many different pieces, including some very rare and hard-to-find serving pieces. This is the famous Denmark pattern (1890 to 1913) in the flow blue based on the Meissen blue onion pattern. Made by Furnivals in Staffordshire England in the late 1800's. After Furnivals stopped making it (circa 1913), the molds were sold to Masons and then to the Franciscan Company. All our pieces are marked with the blue Furnivals backstamp. Beautiful. No chips, no cracks. This auction is for the rare Covered Soup Tureen w/ Ladle.

Winning Bid: $508.^{71}/16

Ended: 10/21/03
History: 124 bids/16
Starting Bid: $9.99 each
Winners: MO, OR, CA, GA, AZ, MI, NY

Viewed
 X

Set of Furnivals China #3

The Story

As I was happily skipping to my car with the hanging lamp, I noticed a box marked "Sango" sitting on one of the tables. I carefully locked the lamp inside my car and went back to take a look. Sango is a manufacturer of dinnerware, but their china is generally not very desirable and I have not had much luck selling it. However, it can never hurt to take a look. When I opened the box I was surprised to find not Sango, but a set of blue and white Furnivals from the 1800's. My heart started racing.

I picked up the box and carried it over to my friend the pricer, Jack, and asked him how much. He said, "How about $5?" Great. I'll take it. As I was walking this box to lock it into the car, I saw the church sale workers putting out another box marked "Sango." Could it be possible? I quickly ran to open that box and found some more of the Furnivals. I decided to wait and see what else they were putting out, and lo and behold out came another box of Furnivals (aka Sango). I paid $10 for the next two boxes for a total of $15. I couldn't believe my luck.

When I got home I found that there were seven soup bowls, seven dinner plates, six salad plates and one each of a creamer, gravy boat, ladle, platter, serving bowl, soup tureen, and egg cup. I was able to break all these out into sixteen different auctions, selling one to two pieces at a time. I do this because

most people are not looking to buy a complete set, but instead want to fill in their existing sets. By doing this, I got over $500 for these auctions!

The moral of this story is, "You can't judge a book by its cover." My grandmother never spent a lot of money on clothes and didn't look like she could afford to spend much when she walked into an antiques or jewelry store. For my wedding, she actually spent $200 on a beaded jacket! It was a shock to all of us, but she looked beautiful.

When she wasn't wearing fancy clothes (99.9% of the time), she was very interested in seeing how shopkeepers would treat her. When they were polite and respectful and she liked what she found, she would pull out a wad of hundred-dollar bills and make their heads spin. If a shop owner was rude or condescending, she would walk out the door and take her business elsewhere. It is a good lesson for all of us. Who would have thought that inside a Sango box would be antique china worth hundreds of dollars?

#4 Smiley Face Teapot

$0.⁵⁰ Paid

From: Church rummage sale

1970's Smiley Face Tea Pot-Yellow-RETRO-CUTE!

Description:
Remember the smiley face in the 1970's? Here is a teapot for you. It is so cute. Yellow with white polka dots. 8" by 5" by 6". Marked "Betallic LLC Made in China." I think it is newer than the 1970's but still very retro. Needs a good cleaning. No chips no cracks. CUTE!

Winning Bid:

$17.²⁷

Ended: 11/1/03
History: 12 bids
Starting Bid: $2.99
Winner: South Dakota

Viewed

000037 X

Smiley Face Teapot #4

The Story

I was still at the same church rummage sale, if you can believe it. Well, I always say that once you find a goldmine, don't rush off. Get it—gold.... rush? Look everything over really well. Anyway, I saw a yellow smiley-face teapot that was marked 50 cents. I am a child of the 1980's. My room was decorated with hearts and rainbows during high school. The bulletin board over my desk was covered with blue and white cloud material with every heart and rainbow known to man attached. I think I have a picture of that somewhere.... So, I just knew that this teapot was retro.

My grandmother always taught me that collecting is cyclical and that everything that was once popular will be popular again. I knew that the 1970's and 1980's were coming back into favor, so I spent 50 cents on the teapot, even though the lid was missing.

After I did the rest of my garage sale route that day, I stopped back by the rummage sale. It's always a good idea when you have found a great sale to check back near the end because prices have generally been slashed, and new treasures may have been uncovered. There on one of the tables, I spotted the yellow teapot lid. I explained to Jack (the same nice pricer) that I had bought the teapot earlier and asked if he would throw in the lid. He said, "Of course." I couldn't believe my luck at this sale!

I put it on eBay with my usual starting price of $9.99 and got no tak-ers. But not to despair; I relisted it the next week at $2.99 and 37 people looked at the auction with the lower price. It ended up getting twelve bids, finally selling for $17.27—more than 34 times what I paid!

The best part of this story is the cute email I received from the buyer. "It is an awesome teapot and it went right on display. I fell in love with it the moment that it came out of the box. I don't think the roommates are going to like it since it's another smiley to add to the collection. Oh well! I don't care what they think."

As my grandmother realized years ago, we are all trying to relive our childhoods by buying things that remind us of our youth. It was true back when she was running her shop and the hot items were Victorian bride's baskets, figural napkin rings and cruets. Some of these items are still in favor, but more and more I see crazy things like cereal boxes, Beanie Babies and smiley face teapots selling for big bucks! Well, maybe not for big bucks, but for at least 34 times their cost. Better odds than Vegas!

This is my bulletin board.

#5 Hutch

$30.00
Paid
From: Garage sale

Antique Secretary/Desk-Hutch-Light Wood-As Is

Description:

This is a beautiful secretary desk/hutch. It is a great project for someone because it has great lines and will be beautiful when restored. 10" deep at the top and 16" deep at the drawers. It is 32" across and 76" tall. The desk is 29" deep when pulled down.

Winning Bid: **$127.50**

Ended: 11/1/03
History: 12 bids
Starting Bid: $9.99
Winner: California

Viewed
 X

The Story

It was almost Halloween and I was madly writing *The 100 Best Things* (trying to get it published by Christmas). In addition, I was still trying to find and sell things on eBay. A girl has to make a living, doesn't she? I had gone to a garage sale in a condo complex and there was this great hutch. The price was only $25. I said to the people having the sale, "If I had a truck, I would buy that in a second." They asked me where I lived and I told them. The wife said, "My husband will drive it to your house for free." "OK," I said, "I'll take it." I paid my $25 and wondered if I would ever see the hutch again.

One reason I liked this piece was that it had shelves and a pull-down desk. My grandmother loved any piece of furniture with cubby holes, secret drawers, writing surfaces or shelves. I knew that she would approve of this piece. I was at a garage sale this past weekend and my mom and I were looking at a piece with a ton of drawers. We both looked at one another and said at the same time, "Grandma would like this."

True to his word, the husband delivered the hutch that afternoon. I gave the gentleman $5 for gas (this was several years ago; today, $5 wouldn't have gotten the hutch around the corner, much less all the way to my house!).

I decided to sell this piece with a fixer upper/as-is angle. A lot of folks on eBay are looking for projects and this can help sell your item. I put it on with a starting bid price of $99 and the notice that it MUST BE PICKED UP. I had many interested buyers email and ask for shipping quotes. They did not read my lips! The shipping to the Midwest was just too exorbitant for a fixer piece. The auction came to an end with no bidders even though 187 people had viewed the auction.

I did not give up and instead relisted it right away with a significantly lower starting price—$9.99. If you can believe it, 404 people looked at it this time and it ended up with 12 bids, finally closing at $127.50 the day after Halloween. By the way, I had the cutest trick or treaters that year.

The couple that bought it drove out from Riverside to pick it up, paid me cash and told me that they planned to paint it a lovely French country blue and use it in their dining room. I made almost $100 on this transaction without ever having to move the item! Those are the kind of deals I like.

#6 Eva Zeisel Coffee Pot

$3.⁰⁰
Paid
From: Charity sale

Eva Zeisel Teapot/Coffee Pot-Haviland White!

Description:
Neat tea pot or coffee pot is signed with 3 paper labels. One says "Eva Zeisel," one says "for Johann Haviland Bavaria Germany," and the last one says "Not Associated with Haviland & Co." It is a white porcelain in excellent condition but could use a cleaning. 7 ½" 6 ½".

Winning Bid:

$63.⁰⁰

Ended: 11/5/03
History: 7 bids
Starting Bid: $9.99
Winner: Mission Hills, CA

Viewed
000059 X

Eva Zeisel Coffee Pot #6

The Story

I started doing Pilates in 1999, about six months before my grandmother died. Pilates is a stretching and toning exercise system that was invented in the 1920's by Joseph Pilates. It is the first exercise that I have ever done that I can't stop doing, and I never get bored with it. I still do Pilates three times a week and I am addicted to it—but at least it is a healthy addiction! It was really a lifesaver for me during the stressful few years after my grandmother passed away when I was liquidating the shop and getting a divorce.

I found a great Pilates studio when I moved to Palm Desert and many of the instructors there have become my friends. When I was driving to my classes that October, I kept seeing a sign for an upcoming charity sale. I was in a private lesson one day when my friend and instructor Kelly Lippert said, "Did you see the sign for that sale? I have been meaning to tell you about it." I told her that I was planning to go that Saturday.

My mom was in town visiting for Halloween, so that Saturday we showed up at 6:45 AM to wait in line. It was freezing! Well, not really, but cold for here—60 degrees. It is always more fun to go yard saling (I just can't bring myself to call it junking) with a friend. It gets lonely when I have to go out by myself. The sale turned out to be incredible. There were tons of great items and my mom and I had a blast!

I bought boxes and boxes and boxes full of great items. The folks running the sale were so nice that they let me make a pile of items behind the checkout table and held on to them for me while I continued to shop. On one of the tables was this pretty white teapot. I had passed it by about eight times because it was priced at $3—a little high for a charity sale. I liked the sleek shape, but had never heard of Eva Zeisel. Haviland is pretty good, though, so I finally decided to take a chance on it. I could tell that there were a lot of quality donations at this sale, and $3 was not too much to risk.

Turned out that Eva is pretty famous. She is known as a prolific ceramics designer who began her career in the 1920's in Hungary—about the same time Pilates was invented. She moved to the United States in 1938, and in 1946 she designed her "Museum" series of modern china. It was an elegant, all-white service in which the pieces had an erect, uplifted look, as if they were growing up from the table. This piece definitely fit the bill. 59 people looked at the teapot, and it sold for more than twenty times what I paid for it.

As my grandmother always said, "You can't go broke making a profit." I know she would have loved to see me make a 2,000% profit!

#7   Watt Pottery Items

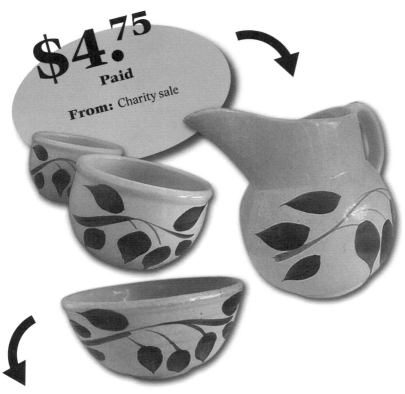

$4.⁷⁵ Paid

From: Charity sale

Watt Pottery Pitcher Tear Drop Leaves-15-NICE

Description:

We have four auctions with Watt pottery up this week. All the auctions are for the red tear drop pattern with 4 green leaves. This is the American Red Bud series. This auction is for the pitcher that is 6" by 4 ¼". Needs a good cleaning. It has a ⅜" by ⅛" nick on the spout. Very slight overall crazing. Signed "Oven Proof USA" or "Oven Ware USA" (can't tell for certain) and a number 15.

Winning Bid: $153.⁰⁹/4

Ended: 11/7/03
History: 40 bids/4
Starting Bid: $9.99 each
Winner: MI, TX, PA

Viewed

000124 X

Watt Pottery Items #7

The Story

I was still at the same charity sale when I spotted some pottery that had no maker's mark. Luckily, I knew immediately what it was from all that time spent with my grandmother in the basement. The basement? Yes, the basement. Every summer we would prepare for our famous yard sales by spending hours pricing items in the basement.

One day, I spotted a pottery cookie jar with hand-painted decorations. The base was signed, "Oven Ware USA." I said to my grandmother, "This looks like it might be good—should we look it up in Schroeder's?" She took one look and said, "I think that is the mark for Watt. Look that up in the pricing guide." My grandmother was so smart. Once she learned something, it was locked in the file cabinet in her mind forever. I miss having all that knowledge just a phone call away.

I used to call her for everything—not just antiques questions, but life questions. I phoned her one day from California and said, "G, how do I boil an egg?" She said, "Please tell me you didn't just call long distance to ask that!" and she laughed that great laugh of hers. She couldn't imagine paying for a phone call over something so trivial. She was much more of a letter writer, and I kept every letter she sent. I have a stack all tied together with antique ribbon and I still enjoy reading them. I used to look for any excuse to call her, even it if was just to see how long to boil an egg. I still don't know how to boil an egg, and with my grandmother gone, I guess I never will.

Watt Pottery was established in Crooks-ville, Ohio, in 1922; it manufactured hand-turned stone containers until 1935. In 1936, Watt began to make common utility kitchenware—mixing bowls, dinnerware and so on. Most Watt ware is hand-painted with bold brush strokes in bright colors that contrast with the natural cream color of the body, and has a very "folk art" look. The factory burned down in 1965 and production ceased.

Ever since that day in my grandmother's basement, I knew to watch out for Watt pieces because there's a high demand for them. They are hard to identify and often will get left on the table after the amateurs sweep through a sale. Many pieces are just signed "ovenware" or stamped with the name of a retail company (because they were made for advertising). There were six pieces at the sale that day, priced at $4.75 for the lot. I scooped them right up. I ended up with four bean cups, a pitcher and a mixing bowl.

After searching eBay, I identified the pattern as "Tear drop." Remember, you must know the pattern name to get the best price. I split the items into four different auctions; the pitcher sold for $46.60, the mixing bowl for $23.49, two bean cups went for $46 and the other two brought in $37. Grand total for these four auctions was over $150. A little knowledge goes a long way.

#8 Cornish Kitchen Ware

Cornish Kitchen Ware TGGreen-RARE Low Pitcher

Description:

We have quite a bit of the Cornish kitchen ware in the blue and white stripe up for auction this week. Most of the auctions have the old mark. The old mark is "TG Green & Co. Ltd. Made in England" in either the green or black shield and banner. I love this pattern. This auction is for a low pitcher which looks like a cereal bowl w/ spout.

Winning Bid: $482.95/18

Ended: 11/7/03
History: 98 bids/18
Starting Bid: $9.99 each
Winner: NY, OR, MD, MA CA, Canada

Viewed

001710 X

Cornish Kitchen Ware   #8

The Story

This was the first thing I bought at that amazing charity sale. I walked in and spotted a box full of blue and white striped Cornish ware immediately. And only $8 for the entire box! Score!

How did I know it was good? Well, let me tell you. During the ten years I was running my grandmother's antiques store, I encountered a few pieces. The couple that I bought them from brought me a magazine article about Cornish ware. It was so interesting and the blue and white pattern was so appealing that I decided to collect it. Oh, no! Not another collection. Well, let me explain. My grandmother was the ultimate collector, if I haven't made that clear yet. She called herself a "shelf collector," because that way, she could have 100 (if not 1,000) collections. She actually kept each collection on a different shelf. Each time I start a new collection, I am just following her example.

When I spotted that box, I knew what a great deal it was. It contained about 40 pieces, and at a price of only $8, each piece was less than 25 cents. I will always try dinnerware sets if I can pick up the pieces for under $1 each. But this set was particularly good—the pieces were all in great condition, and they were in an older, very collectible style. I quickly put the box in my pile behind the cashier's desk so that no one else would grab it.

Cornish ware was made by the TG Green Company at their Church Gresley Pottery in the Staffordshire section of England beginning in the 1920's. TG Green made a wide range of this blue and white banded pottery and they are still producing it today. Most older Cornish ware—which is much more collectible than the newer pieces—has either a black or green shield backstamp (a signature on the back or bottom of an item). This dates it from the late 1920's to the late 1960's. All my pieces had this older mark. Yippeee!

I sell a lot of dinnerware on eBay and I make a lot of money doing this. I have learned that serving pieces usually sell for the most, but you can't give away cups and saucers. My storeroom is full of lonely cups and saucers, while the plates, bowls and serving pieces have all found loving homes. People don't use cups and saucers much anymore, so there just isn't a demand.

I always break the dinner sets out into auctions of one to four pieces. You get more money by not selling as a set. With the Cornish ware, I made eighteen different auctions, consisting of groupings like three mugs, two egg cups, one platter, and four cups and saucers. I was hoping that by offering four cups and saucers together (instead of two) that they might sell.

Interestingly enough, the four cups and saucers actually sold! I got $36.76 for them, and altogether, the box (broken out into eighteen auctions) brought in $482! It was an amazing return on my investment—over 6,000%. I love my job!

#9 Chintz Condiment Set

Ascot Crown Ducal Chintz OLD 4pc Condiment Set

Description:
This is the most darling antique piece of chintz. I would date it to the 1920's to 1930's. It is signed "Crown Ducal Ware England." It is 5 ¼" by 4 ¼" by 3 ⅛". A super nice eBayer has let us know that this is the Ascot pattern! There are 4 pieces: the main base which looks like it is for an open salt cellar, the removable pepper shaker, the mustard lid and the mustard base which also comes out. Floral pattern in pinks, blues and greens.

Winning Bid:

$99.⁰⁰

Ended: 11/8/03
History: 1 bid
Starting Bid: $99
Winner: Canada

Viewed

000124 X

Chintz Condiment Set #9

The Story

That same charity sale had several tables set up as a "boutique" section. Typically, I check boutique areas last, because if people think that an item is "boutique" quality, it will usually be too expensive. When I finally headed to the boutique tables, I found a chintz piece priced at $15. Chintz, a layered floral design that's been popular for over 200 years, is very collectible, but $15 is high.

In 1998, I sold a chintz side teapot for over $1,000 (see #2 in the first *100 Best* book), but eBay has grown a lot since then and chintz has become more readily accessible. I decided to buy it anyway, but when I got it home and starting researching it, I couldn't find the pattern name anywhere. So I listed it on eBay with a high starting price— $199—and used the auction title to ask for help. Usually, a nice eBayer will let me know pretty quickly what I have, and I can update the title and the description. I deliberately set a high starting price for an item if I can't fully identify it be-

cause this ensures a reasonably good price. Then, I can always relist the item at a lower starting bid if it doesn't sell.

Right after the auction began, I got an email from "Diane" in Canada. She told me the pattern was "Ascot," and although it is not popular with other chintz collectors, it was her favorite. She wanted me to consider adding a

"Buy It Now" feature so she could just pay for the condiment set and skip the bidding process. My policy is to never end auctions early, so I had to tell her no. But with her information, I was able to change the auction title to include the pattern name "Ascot."

The funny part of this story is that I recognized Diane's name from her email. When I had sold the chintz side teapot many years earlier, she was the eBayer who had helped me identify the pattern. She had told me then that if the side teapot had been Ascot, she would have bid in a minute and probably mortgaged the house for it.

After doing more research, I decided that the condiment set was worth $199 and I would leave it at that price. I waited seven days for the auction to end but no one bid. In retrospect, I should have taken Diane's $199 offer—but you just never know. I relisted the mustard at a $99 starting price and got only one bid—Diane's! She got a bargain and I still made money. It was probably her good karma for being so nice and helping me identify the teapot pattern so many years ago. Speaking of good karma, my grandmother left quite a legacy. Indiana was only 1 ½ when her great grandma died, but she still remembers her. About the time I was listing this piece, she drew this wonderful picture to honor her.

#10 Boopie Burple Glasses

$8.00
Paid
From: Charity sale

3 Green Anchor Hocking Burple Ice Tea Glasses

Description:

I think this is the Anchor Hocking Inspiration (nicknamed Burple) pattern. If not, please let me know. These lovely forest green glasses were produced by AH from the mid-1940's until the early 1960's. Unlike AH's other Boopie (Berwick line) and Bubble (Early American line) of glassware, which had 32 or 40 pieces in a service for eight, these Burple glasses in Forest Green have 48 pieces.

Winning Bid: **$223.⁴³/₉**

Ended: 11/11/03
History: 58 bids/9
Starting Bid: $9.99 each
Winners: TX, GA, AL, OK, MS, LA

Viewed

000819 X

The Story

I am still at that same charity sale. I bet you wish that I would leave already. Enough, enough! This is the last of five items that I am going to talk about that I bought at that one sale, but I found even more that I am not writing about. These amazing sales come along once in a great while and when you find one, do not leave! And for heaven's sake—go back on Sunday.

I didn't buy these glasses the first day of the sale. I bought them on Sunday afternoon. Everyone else had passed them over also! My ex-husband takes my kids Friday night and Saturday mornings so that I can garage sale. It was Sunday afternoon and my mom was visiting. I said to her, "You know, that sale was so amazing yesterday—I think we should go take one more peek." Always ready for an adventure, we grabbed the kids and headed back to the sale.

I gave Houston and Indy $5 each to spend, so off they went. Houston found a huge umbrella that we could use to keep the sun off of us at baseball games, and Indy found an Easter decoration. It didn't matter that Easter was five months away—my daughter loves holidays!

I walked in and saw that these green glasses were still on a table. 22 pieces of stemware for a total of $8. I thought, those can't be antique or collectible, but it is less than 40 cents apiece—why not? So I bought them and the kids helped me pack them up. They love it when I take them to sales and let them help (especially when I let them spend MY money!).

I got the glasses home and did my research. Turns out they were very collectible! I found that they were made by Anchor Hocking (abbreviated as "AH") in the 1940's to the 1960's and they were the Inspiration pattern (also called "Burple"). Where did that name come from? AH made quite a few stemware patterns with bubbles; of those, three are known as Boopie, Bubble and Burple. A little too confusing for this girl! Anchor Hocking was born of a merger of the Hocking Glass and the Anchor Cap Company in 1937. They are still in operation today, and you might know them best for their Fire King line of glass dinnerware.

I put the stemware on eBay in nine separate auctions and couldn't believe it when my $8 investment turned into $223.43! It is definitely worth revisiting a good sale on the last day.

#11 Walt Disney Art

Walt Disney Autograph 1950s RARE Original Art

Description:

This is an amazing piece of Disney Memorabilia. It is a "get well" card hand-inked and painted by the Disney Art Props Department. I bought this from a man and his mother who worked for Disney circa 1950's. The center art portion is 15" by 10 ¼" and is so neat. It shows Pluto, Mickey Mouse, Goofy crying, Donald Duck, and Chip n' Dale around a big pot of flowers with a sign that says "Best Wishes from all of your friends at Disney." It is signed by about 88 Disney Employees including at the very top WALT DISNEY!!

Winning Bid: $2,750.^{00}

Ended: 11/15/03
History: 24 bids
Starting Bid: $9.99/$999 reserve
Winner: Idaho

Viewed

000629 X

Walt Disney Art #11

The Story

October of 2003 was a wonderful month for me on eBay. Not only did I score big at that charity sale, but I found the item that I would sell on eBay for the most money so far in my career!

A friend had told me about an amazing neighborhood sale in a gated community here in Palm Desert, so off I went. The cars were lined up down the block waiting for the gates to open. Not a good sign. The first garage I entered was full of artwork. I know nothing about art, and a gentleman was already there negotiating to buy most of it.

While he was making an offer for all the large paintings, I took a look around. Against the back wall was a Disney print. My kids love Disneyland, so I asked, "How much?" "Twenty dollars," was the reply. The other buyer argued, "I already bought that! It was included with all of this." The man running the sale said, "No, it wasn't." I said, "Great, I'll take it!" and paid quickly so I could leave before a riot broke out!

As I was heading back to my car, the man running the sale stopped me to tell me a little bit about the piece I had just purchased. He and his mother had been animators for the Disney Company in the 1950's and 1960's, and when his mom got sick, the animation department drew this and signed the matting around the picture. It wasn't a print after all, but an original Disney drawing! Wow! I had bought it with the idea of giving it to my son, Houston, but I decided to rethink that plan.

When I finally arrived home, I set the picture down and looked at it more closely. I felt goosebumps rising on my arms as I noticed that there was a very big and famous signature on the top of the picture. Walt Disney himself had signed the matting!

I did a little research and found that a Walt Disney signature alone can sell for $500 to $1,000, and I had a unique piece. It was so exciting. I showed it to Houston when he got home. Big mistake. He decided right then and there that he wanted this drawing more than life itself. I told him that I needed to sell it to pay the mortgage, but that some day when I could afford it, I would buy him a Walt Disney autograph.

As a consolation, I took it in to school and let him share it with his class. Mr. Carroll, his wonderful second grade teacher, is a garage-saler like myself. He got such a kick out of it!

I did a lot of research on this piece, identifying each of the signatures. I included each and every name in the listing (which I had to shorten a lot to fit in this book). I put a reserve of $999 on this piece and was overjoyed when it sold for $2,750!!! By the way, Houston reminds me every month or so that I owe him a Disney signature. Will I ever learn?

#12 Strawberry Necklace

$0.⁰⁰ Paid

From: Inheritance - sold on consignment for Lee

Vintage Plastic-Bakelite Strawberry Necklace!

Description:

This vintage plastic necklace is green and red. I think the green is plastic and the red may be bakelite or catalin. It has a different feel from the other plastic. It looks like strawberries and leaves. It is very cute. There are 9 red berries and 9 green leaves times two. 14" around and in very good condition.

Winning Bid:

$40.⁰⁰

Ended: 12/2/03
History: 7 bids
Starting Bid: $9.99
Winner: California

Viewed

000062 X

Strawberry Necklace #12

The Story

As you know, my brother, sister, and mom all inherited tons of stuff—literally—from my grandmother when she passed away. We each got about 100 huge boxes filled with memories, pieces of our hearts, and items to sell. Every time I opened one, I was taken back to days spent in the shop with my grandmother. It always left me feeling sad, nostalgic and bittersweet all at the same time.

The amazing thing was, we had no idea what would be inside a box when we opened it. Sometimes we would find personal items from my grandmother (I got her watch in one—it still sits on my desk). Sometimes we would just find paperwork from the antiques store, or glassware and jewelry to sell. Opening those boxes was like going on a treasure hunt.

I went through about 60 of my boxes when I first moved back to California because I didn't want to go out to garage sales every weekend. I was talking to my good friend Peter one night about how sad it would be when all the boxes were gone. He said, "Dralle, stop right now—do not open any more boxes. You want those to last forever. Let yourself open one box a month and focus on selling things from garage sales. Hey, why don't you see if you can buy the boxes from the rest of your family?" He was (and is) brilliant!

I immediately called everyone, and no one wanted to sell. I couldn't blame them—we all loved my grandmother dearly and the boxes were our last ties to her. My brother did have an idea. He said, "Why don't you sell some of my things for me and I'll pay you a commission?" "How about 50%?" My brother knows how labor-intensive eBay is, and he knew that I wasn't going to do it for any less. Great! We struck a deal.

One of the first items I sold for him was this plastic strawberry necklace. It had only been in the shop for the last few months before we closed, when everything was up to 70% off. So this necklace, although marked at $25, could have been bought for $7.50. It hadn't sold even at that price, so we gave it a whirl on eBay.

I started it at $9.99 and called it a vintage plastic/bakelite necklace. There are a lot of both strawberry and bakelite collectors. Bakelite and catalin are early forms of plastic, invented in 1908 and popular from the 1930's to 1950's. Bakelite was typically molded, dark in color, and used for utilitarian pieces. Catalin was cast and used mostly for jewelry and novelties. The leaves on this piece were definitely just ordinary plastic, but the strawberries seemed like catalin. Bakelite, however, is the term more commonly known by collectors, so that is what I used in the title.

This piece got seven bids and ended up selling for $40! The best part was that I got $20 for selling it for my brother without investing any money or time to go out and hunt for it. A win-win situation!

#13 Halcyon Days Clock

$2.00 Paid
From: Garage sale

Halcyon Days Battersea RED Leopard Clock-MIB!

Description:

This is a wonderful Halcyon Days Enamel Battersea Red Leopard Clock. It comes mint in the original box with three certificates of authenticity. It is a quartz desk alarm clock. It measures 1 ¾" by 2" by ⅜". It is in excellent condition and looks like it was never used. The nice box is 4" by 3" by 2 ¾".

Winning Bid: **$102.50**

Ended: 12/3/03
History: 9 bids
Starting Bid: $9.99
Winner: Texas

Viewed
 X

Halcyon Days Clock #13

The Story

I was out garage saling on the morning of the big USC vs. UCLA game and I was wearing a USC shirt. I did my undergraduate and graduate degrees there, so I am a serious fan. "Your blood doesn't run red, it runs cardinal," my dad tells me (our colors are cardinal and gold).

On Saturdays when I don't have anyone to treasure hunt with me, I make myself go to at least ten garage sales before heading home. To make my quota, I had to go to a sale in one of the worst parts of town. Actually, there are no "worst" parts of town here in Palm Desert, but this sale was in an area where I typically don't find much. The items at this sale were strewn all over the ground and there weren't very many smalls.

"Smalls" is an old-time antiques dealer word for smaller items that are easily packed. My grandmother and her friends used this term a lot when we were at antiques shows. I do most of my business in smalls, but at this garage sale, I only saw two of them. They were on the table next to the woman running the sale. She smiled when she saw my shirt. "USC! I'm an alum—are you?" I said I was, and we started chatting about the game coming up that afternoon. One of the two smalls looked interesting. It was a clock in its original box, marked "Halcyon Days." I knew that this was a good brand, so I asked her how much she wanted for it. She replied, "Since you are a fellow alum, how about $2?" Sold!

This Halcyon Days piece was in a style called "Battersea," and I knew that Battersea hinged boxes are very desirable—but I knew nothing about Battersea clocks. It was mint in the original box, however, and you can't lose much on a $2 investment.

As I researched my find, I discovered that Battersea is the name for enamel-on-metal wares that have been made in England since 1750. Halcyon Days is a newer company, and has only been producing Battersea since 1950. Oddly enough, my grandmother started her antiques store in 1950!

The Halcyon Days Company has some cachet with collectors because it is warranted as a supplier of *objets d'art* to the British royal family. Their wares are made by craftspeople in Bilston, the traditional English center of enameling on copper. The company web site claims that its goods are "prized by collectors all over the word as 'small' works of art." They are, it says, "the antiques of tomorrow." Score! Somehow, this entire transaction had my grandmother written all over it—the same opening year (1950), the use of the term "small" on the Halcyon Days website, the phrase "antiques of tomorrow" . . . . Coincidence?—I think not.

I always look for Halcyon Days items now when I am out. I haven't run across one since. That $2 clock sold for over $100 on eBay!

#14 Cribbage Board

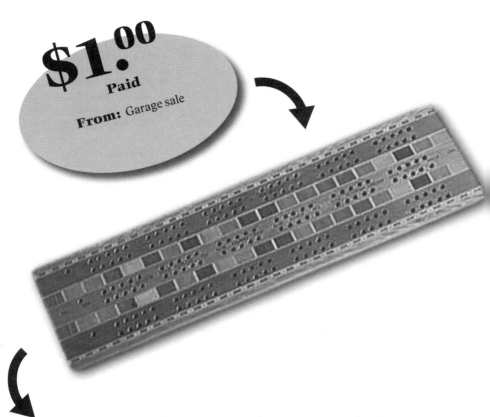

$1.00 Paid

From: Garage sale

New Zealand Cribbage Board-Sovereign-Timbers!

Description:
New Zealand Cribbage Board is 12" by 3" by ¾". Made in New Zealand by Sovereign. It shows the native woods of New Zealand: Silver Pin, Tawa, Tawhai, Pukatea, Totara, Z, Towaii, Kauri, Maire, Rata. In great condition but no lids for the pegs on the back and no pegs. Vintage.

Winning Bid:

$76.00

Ended: 12/9/03
History: 19 bids
Starting Bid: $9.99
Winner: Idaho

Viewed
 X

Cribbage Board #14

The Story

I was at a yard sale one morning that had items strewn haphazardly all over the ground and on tables. Everything was either dirty or in plastic bags and I did not want to touch anything. To find the treasures, though, you have to get your hands dirty. Just don't forget to wash them when you get home!

I took a deep breath and started rifling through the nearest pile of things. It turned out to be quite an eclectic collection of stuff, and seemed to come from locations all over the world. On one of the tables was this cribbage board. It wasn't in great shape because it was missing the pegs and the back cover. It was only $1, though, so I bought it.

Vintage games, toys and dolls are all very desirable on eBay. I will say this again and again just so that it sinks in: people are trying to buy their childhoods. We all remember those carefree days of our youth, and items that bring back those days make us feel great. We will bid higher and higher for them.

Do you remember coming home from school, grabbing your bike, and roaming the neighborhood playing for hours until dinner? I had a pink girl's bike with a banana seat and I loved it! I got it for my sixth birthday and I rode it to my first day of school at Monmouth Elementary in Oregon.

We lived at 700 Sacre Lane, and I can still picture myself standing in front of our house in the wild "Op Art" blue dress that my mom made for me to wear on that special day. I bet that dress would bring some big money on eBay these days! By the way, those banana bikes from the 1970's can sell for over $1,000 in great condition, and just the banana seat alone can bring $75.

But I digress (and I had so much fun doing it!). Let's get back to the cribbage board. Cribbage is a game played with cards and a board with pegs; it was invented by a British poet in the early seventeenth century. Cribbage has survived several hundred years with no major changes as one of the most popular games in the English-speaking world. Who knew? The cribbage board itself is used only for scoring; it is made up of a series of holes (streets) on which points are tallied with pegs.

When I got home and looked at the board closer, I found a label that explained that the inlaid portions had been made of the ten different types of wood indigenous to New Zealand. It was really lovely. I put it on eBay with a starting bid price of $9.99.

I couldn't believe it, but 131 people looked at this auction and it got nineteen bids. It turned out to be a really desirable piece that people wanted—I assume to help them remember a trip to New Zealand or perhaps their New Zealand roots. It sold for $76. I like making $75 on items I sell on eBay. It really makes digging through other people's castoffs (OPC) worth it!

#15 3 Sterling Napkin Rings

$1.⁰⁰ **Paid**

From: Garage sale

Edna Sterling 38 Antique Napkin Ring-Fancy!!

Description:

Beautiful Napkin Ring is marked Sterling 38. It has a fancy and ornate edge—Art Nouveau. It is 1 ⅜" by 1 ⅝". Engraved with the name "Edna." Antique 1890's to 1920's and in very good condition. It will polish up better than the photo shows.

Winning Bid: **$122.⁰⁰/₃**

Ended: 12/10/03
History: 26 bids/3
Starting Bid: $9.99 each
Winners: NJ, OH, DE

Viewed
000255 X

The Story

I was still at that filthy yard sale with my mom, who was finally in town for good. She had decided to try living in Palm Desert so that she could be closer to her grandkids—always a good idea, in my opinion. She was staying with us until she could decide exactly where to live.

It was the weekend after Thanksgiving and my brother and sister were also in town. It is always fun to spend the holidays with my awesome family. Lee and Kristin were watching the kids so that we could go out and garage sale. Surprisingly, there were quite a few sales that Saturday.

I had already decided to buy the cribbage board when I spotted a big Ziploc baggie full of kitchen utensils and what looked like napkin rings. It was so dirty that I was hesitant to open the bag. I asked the price, and the lady said $1. I figured I couldn't go wrong with that price—and I would just wear rubber gloves when I sorted through it.

Napkin rings, cruets, and toothpick holders are some of the items that my grandmother's generation collected. When Lee, Kristin and I were little, my grandmother started collections for all of us. If you can believe it, I was just seven and a half when we three appeared with our collections in "Silver Magazine." I collected silver napkin rings and bells with people on them, my brother col-

Lee Alan Dralle, age 5 collects Canadian Silver Dollars and Bells with animals on them.

Kristin Kay Dralle, age 1½ collects spoons with animals and nursery rhymes. She also has a collection of Canadian Silver Dollars, not shown.

Lynn Adelle Dralle is age 7½. She collects Canadian Silver Dollars, Silver Napkin Rings and Bells with People on them.

lected animal-themed bells, and my sister collected spoons with animals and nursery rhymes on them. My grandma had started a collection of Canadian silver dollars for each of us, which she viewed as our college funds. She would never put money in the bank when she could buy collectibles that had a much better chance of appreciating. All three of us did use those coins later to fund our college educations. Smart Grandma!

Anyway, the point of this story is that because of that early collection, I knew that sterling and even silver plate napkin rings could bring in a lot of money. When I got home, I found three napkin rings mixed in with dirty kitchen utensils (which I threw away). Much to my surprise and delight, all three of the napkin rings were marked sterling! What a bonanza.

I put them on eBay in three separate auctions. The most ornate napkin ring, inscribed "Edna," sold for $66. The more modern-looking Gorham napkin ring (marked "William") sold for $41. The plain round one with the initials "WMS" sold for only $15. It would appear that names sell better than just initials. Any way you slice it, I was thrilled with the three of them selling for $122. My grandmother would have been so proud!

#16 Corkscrew

Figural Corkscrew Cellar Master-Double Lever-WOW

Description:
Really neat figural cork screw corkscrew or wine opener is 8" by 2". It is silverplate and looks to be in excellent condition. It appears to be a monk who is also the sommelier or cellar master as he has the wine cellar key around his neck. Double lever and very cute.

Winning Bid: **$113.⁶²**

Ended: 12/30/03
History: 7 bids
Starting Bid: $9.99
Winner: Australia

Viewed

000125 X

The Story

It was a few weeks before Christmas and my dad was in town visiting. He came to help me take care of my kids and to celebrate my daughter's 5th birthday. One Friday morning, I dragged him along with me to a strange garage sale. He spent most of the time taking a nap in my car and snoring loudly—which he does quite well.

It was an estate sale at a business on the outskirts of town. There were buildings and buildings full of things. Most of the stuff was in boxes that were scattered all around in the dirt. Everything was filthy and nothing looked like it was going to bring in much money. I did pick out a few items, however, and ended up throwing in this wine opener. I think they charged me 50 cents or $1.

I got him home and did some research. There are a lot of collectors for corkscrews, if you can believe it! I guess what I am finding is that there are collectors for anything you can imagine. I found that a similar corkscrew had sold for $23.83 within the last few weeks—not a bad return for a buck! My research also showed that this was a double-levered corkscrew and the fact that the monk's arms were the levers made it especially appealing.

I also learned that the monk was probably a sommelier. "Sommelier" is a French term for a wine steward. A wine steward is a restaurant employee who is responsible for helping diners select an appropriate

wine for each course, and for opening, decanting and serving the wine. What was really neat was that there was a key around the monk's neck, which would have been the key to unlock the wine cellar. I included this interesting information in the listing.

An old-fashioned term that I learned from my grandmother is "figural." She would often describe items with this term. She would say, "Look at my figural toothpick holder collection," or "You collect figural napkin rings." Figural means "consisting of or forming human or animal figures." It is a great term to use in your listings, as there are many people who collect figural items. I used "figural" in this title, which I think increased the number of times the auction was viewed.

When I went to list this item, I found that corkscrews have their very own category on eBay: "Collectibles > Barware > Corkscrews." I listed it in this category and started the bidding at $9.99. It got seven bids and sold for $113.62. I couldn't believe it—especially since a similar one had only gone for $23.83! It is amazing to me that on eBay, the same item one week will only sell for $23 and the next week it will sell for over $110! And it got shipped to Australia. The user ID of the buyer was so cute—it was something like Oz-Screw. He is from Oz (Australia) and he collects corkscrews. You can't make up stuff like this!

#17 Whale Snuff Box

$16.00
Shop Paid
From: Gift Show

Scrimshaw Orca Whale Snuff Box-Bone/Ivory-WOW

Description:
This is a darling scrimshaw snuff or other type of hinged box. It has an orca whale raised on the top and whales and fish on the sides. It is bone or ivory. 2 ⅝" by 1 ⅛" by 1". It is so cute and from the 1980's.

Winning Bid: **$69.00**

Ended: 12/30/03
History: 14 bids
Starting Bid: $9.99
Winner: Washington

Viewed
 X

Whale Snuff Box   #17

The Story

Growing up with a grandmother who had operated a store since 1950 always made for interesting adventures. When my grandma opened her shop, she named it "Cheryl Leaf Antiques, Gifts & Coins." She knew from the get-go that just carrying antiques was not enough. She was so smart, and I will always be grateful for all the wonderful lessons she taught me. She had a way of teaching without cramming anything down my throat. She worked hard, treated people well and always enjoyed her life. I try to follow her example every day.

Twice a year Seattle hosted a huge gift show. It was the place local retailers went to purchase gift and jewelry items wholesale. My grandmother wouldn't miss a gift show for the world. She always made a huge day out of it. She would invite any of us that wanted to go.

On the morning of the gift show, my grandma would get up at her usual 5 AM to start making sandwiches for the trip. She would never let anyone go hungry but wouldn't think of actually spending her hard-earned money on restaurant food, either. Ham and cheese on wheat bread was her specialty, and she would have a bread bag filled to the top by the time we left for Seattle at 7 AM.

To get to the show, we would all pile into her brown Chevy van. It only had two seats, so if more than two were going, she would put a bench (without a seat belt or back rest) between the two front seats. If more than three people wanted to make the trip, she would put an armchair or two in the back and away we would go. Back in the day, we could get away with this. Amazingly scary!

We would spend all day walking the floors at the Seattle center. Her favorite area at the gift show was the upstairs section that housed all the jewelry. It was called the Vault. She would spend thousands of dollars (usually cash) with the jewelry vendors. Sometimes on the way home, as a special treat, my grandmother would stop in Marysville at the pie house. Those were the days!

It was on one of these trips in the 1980's that she bought an assortment of hinged boxes. This one did not sell in the shop and I inherited it. The box was still marked with a $32 price tag from the gift show, so she probably paid the dealers' price of $16 for it.

I put the whale box on eBay with a starting bid of $9.99 and stated that I wasn't sure if it was bone or ivory. Natural ivory has crosshatches that distinguish it from bone, but they can be faint, and I couldn't tell for sure so I listed it using both terms. I was very happy when it sold for $69! The funny thing was that I had hauled it from Washington to California (when I moved) and it ended up going back to a tiny suburb of Seattle, all because of eBay. I guess that is where it belongs.

#18 Cloisonné Stamp Box

$5.00 Paid

From: Garage sale

Cloisonné Stamp Box-Old-DARLING-Blue/Yellow!

Description:

Really neat Cloisonné stamp box is marked "China." It is from the 1920's to 1940's. It is blue and yellow with a green enamel interior. It is 4 ¾" by 1 ¼" by 1 ½". It has divided compartments. In excellent condition.

Winning Bid: **$74.99**

Ended: 12/30/03
History: 13 bids
Starting Bid: $9.99
Winner: Nevada

Viewed

 **X**

Cloisonné Stamp Box #18

The Story

I bought this box at a garage sale in Palm Springs. We rarely venture over to Palm Springs because it is half an hour away and I typically find better items in Palm Desert. It was the week before Christmas, however, and there were not very many sales, so my Mom and I were forced to check out all the Palm Springs listings.

The sale where I found this box was very strange. Aren't all garage sales strange on some level? You are entering another person's personal space and looking at the parts of their lives that they want to discard. Oh, well—it is a job hazard. This sale had thousands of items spread out in the driveway and in the garage. Things were priced high and I thought that maybe the people running the sale were dealers.

This box was marked $5. Not cheap, but not overly expensive. The box had two things going for it. It was made of cloisonné (enamel on wire metalwork), and it was designed to hold postage stamps. The divided sections inside had a curved base so that your finger could easily grasp the stamp you needed. Desk items like inkwells, antique fountain pens, and ink blotters are very collectible, as is cloisonné. I decided to take a chance on it.

I put this item up for sale in an auction that ended close to New Year's Day. I needed some pocket change because I was going to the Rose Bowl!!! My USC Trojans were in the BCS National Championship and I had tickets.

My best friend from high school, Melanie Souve, was in town and we were really excited to go to the game. We drove into LA early that morning and checked into our hotel, The New Otani. We headed over to Pasadena and watched USC trounce Michigan. It was such a fun day! We went out for sushi in Little Tokyo after the game. This cloisonné box ended up paying for our dinner!

The final bid in that auction was almost $75, by a gentleman who had bought a ton of stuff from us. On eBay we often get repeat customers, but every once in a great while we get a SERIOUS repeat customer. You have got to love someone who keeps coming back for more.

"Simplys" (name changed to protect the innocent) was that customer for us. He would buy about six items at a time and ask for a combined invoice. He lasted almost a year as our most loyal customer on record. Then one day we simply stopped hearing from him. We don't know what happened to him. I still miss Simplys. I think he spent between $2,000 and $3,000 with us. Gone are the days of wine and roses. I am still looking for my next Simplys. They come along once in a blue moon.

#19 Misha Bear

$0.^{00} Paid

From: Inheritance - sold on consignment for Lee

Misha Bear 1980 Olympics MWT-Russian-RARE!

Description:
This Misha bear has the belt and original tags. It is 13" and was made for the Moscow Russian Olympics in 1980 that the US did not attend. He was made by Dakin and these are getting harder and harder to find in good condition. He is in very good shape.

Winning Bid:

$66.^{00}

Ended: 1/7/04
History: 26 bids
Starting Bid: $9.99
Winner: France

Viewed
 X
000084

Misha Bear #19

The Story

I was still selling items for my brother and in one of his boxes was this bear. It brought back memories of the shop, my grandma and the attic. The attic? What am I talking about? My grandmother had been tucking things away in the attic above her shop since 1950. It had layers upon layers of things in it; rifling through it was like going on an archeological dig. It was always a dream of my grandmother's to sort that attic. When she added on her big addition in the early 1970's, she even built a sorting room that opened up right into the attic. Sadly, we never managed to get the attic sorted until after she passed away.

She would often say to us, "What are you guys going to do with all this junk when I am gone?" And then she would laugh that great laugh of hers because she knew it wasn't junk—and that going through it would be a nearly impossible task. She would also say to me, "Now, don't you give this stuff away for pennies on the dollar." Talk about pressure.

So why did that bear remind me of the attic? Well, in the 1980's, the US decided to boycott the Russian Olympics for political reasons. Misha was the mascot of those Olympics, and not many Misha plush bears were manufactured because of the boycott. My grandmother was at an antiques show in Oregon when the boycott was announced, and she quickly hit every major toy store in town so she could buy up all the Mishas. She decided to store them

(instead of selling them right away) because she knew that they would be worth more in the future. I was in high school at the time and worked for her every Saturday and many afternoons after school. Guess who got to stuff the 50 Misha bears into big black garbage bags and carry them up into the attic? Me!

Do you see why it is so hard for me to sell things from my past? Everything has a connection to my grandmother. I still miss her dearly and regret that we didn't find a way to keep the building that housed not only the antiques store, but also her home. I know it's silly, but I think about that magical place a lot. It is hard to lose both a person and a place that have had such an impact on your life.

I just got through reading my Christmas cards from this year. So many of my grandmother's friends and customers said things like, "Your grandmother would be so proud of you." If only she were still here—she would be almost 94 years old. This is making me cry, so let's get back to Misha. This bear got 26 bids and ended up selling for $66! He now lives in France. How exciting for him!

#20 Lamp Mechanism

Antique Library/Parlor Lamp Part-Raises/Lower

Description:
This is a part for an antique library or parlor hanging lamp. It is the raising and lowering mechanism that was used to make it easier to light the flame/wick. I don't know what it is called. It is definitely antique—1880's or so. It is 5" by 3 ½" by 4 ¾" and needs work. It is stiff, tarnished and rusty.

Winning Bid: $49.00

Ended: 1/14/04
History: 4 bids
Starting Bid: $9.99
Winner: Kansas

Viewed
 X

The Story

This was one of those auctions that made my assistant Mari and I look at each other and say, "Huh?" It was definitely a head-scratcher. I knew that this was a rare antique lamp part when I pulled it out of one of my boxes from the shop, but it was in horrendous condition.

When I teach about eBay, I always tell my classes that "good condition sells" and that "condition is everything" and then I tell them, "the rule is the exception on eBay." The reason I add that last part is because just when I think I have eBay all figured out, something like this big heavy piece of rusted metal will go and sell for almost $50!

Check out my description. I say "Needs work. It is stiff, tarnished and rusty." Hardly makes you want to spend $1 for it, much less $50.

Let me tell you more about why I think it sold for so much. In Victorian times, before electricity, parlor or library lamps

were used for light in the fancy sitting rooms (please see story #2 to see what a full lamp looks like). Victorian lamps were typically hung high up, near the ceiling. Lighting them was a challenge unless a raising and lowering mechanism was used. These mechanisms had chain wrapped around them and worked like large pulleys. By using the mechanism, the lamp could easily be raised and lowered so that the wick could be lit or blown out.

I would imagine that not many of these mechanisms survived. They weren't the prettiest part of the lamp, and many probably became rusty like this one (since they were made of iron and not brass). Most were probably thrown away because of their condition or because of the fact that most people wouldn't know what they were used for.

Boy, did my grandmother know her lamp parts. Second only to jewelry, lamps and lamp making were her passion. The entire huge basement at her house and shop was filled from floor to ceiling with lamp parts—chimneys, shades, wicks, burners, rods, columns, prisms, chain, frames, and so on. I was taught from a very early age to value all these pieces. I didn't ever understand how they all fit together, but she sure did. My grandmother could assemble a lamp out of what looked like nothing to me and before you knew it—there it was hanging up for sale in the shop. She really was amazing.

I couldn't believe that 132 people looked at this auction. It only got four bids, but that was enough to drive up the price. My grandmother would have gotten such a kick out of this part selling for so much money.

#21 Grocery Store Lids

$0.00 Paid

From: Inheritance

Antique Drug/Candy Store Apothecary Jar Lid

Description:
This is a great antique large grocery store, drug store or candy store apothecary jar lid. It is antique—1900's or so. It is rough around the base but no chips. There is a line in the making. 6 ⅝" at the inner rim and 7 ⅞" to the outside edge and 2 ¾" tall. Probably for a flour, candy or sugar jar that would have sat on the shelf in an old-time store.

Winning Bid:

$71.²⁵/₂

Ended: 1/16/04
History: 14 bids/2
Starting Bid: $9.99 each
Winner: RI, GA

Viewed
000183 X

Grocery Store Lids #21

The Story

I had spent the 4th quarter of 2003 madly writing *The 100 Best Things I've Sold on eBay*. It turned out to be the greatest thing I had ever written (if I do say so myself). I was so proud of that book. It forced me to use my writing skills—skills I didn't even know I had. English was one of my most difficult subjects in both high school and college. Never in a million years did I picture myself becoming a successful author. It still amazes me that I have been published by Scholastic, McGraw-Hill and John Wiley & Sons.

The 100 Best gave me a chance to pour my heart out, be creative and really tell my grandmother's story. The first copies were ready right before the New Year, so I sent them out with my Christmas cards to 200 friends and family. I also sent the book to some of the buyers of the 100 items. Most people received it mid-January, just as I was putting these two jar lids up for sale on eBay.

Immediately, the comments started rolling in by email. I was overwhelmed that others felt so positive about the book and (more importantly) about my grandmother.

"What a great project—both as a book and as a wonderful way to honor your grandmother. She was quite a terrific woman, but then so are you. I really enjoyed reading about your adventures. Congrats!" (Reed McColm, Post Falls, ID)

"You have done a MARVELOUS job of bringing your tales to life—and we think the format is outstanding. How proud your grandmother would be to see what you have done!!" (The Herretts, Defiance, OH; buyers of #4, Kewpies)

"Thank you so much for the book. I couldn't put it down and have read it from cover to cover twice already! It was very entertaining and I wanted it to go on and on." (Kay Faulkner, Ferndale, WA)

"The 100 Best is fantastic and a great tribute to your grandmother. I couldn't put your book down." (Jim Leno, W. Brookefield, MA; buyer of #8, Scrooge)

In one of the boxes that I inherited from that wonderful lady who so inspired me and many others, I found two old grocery or drug store lids. I always tell my classes and write in my books that sometimes the parts will sell for more than the whole. If you had the entire jar with the lid, you might not get as much as I did for these two orphans. The reason seems to be that people can be more motivated to fix the things they already own (which may have sentimental value) than to buy new things.

That was the case with these lids, and they ended up selling for over $70. I got $36.66 for one and $34.59 for the other. Amazing!—just like the response to *The 100 Best*.

#22 Chanel Sunglasses

$5.00 Paid

From: Garage sale

Chanel Sunglasses-MIB-02466/26-Vintage-NICE!

Description:

This is a great pair of Chanel Sunglasses marked "Made in Italy" and "02466 26." They come mint with the original box and black cover. MIB stands for "mint in box." They look barely used. Faux tortoise with gold. The box is 1 ¾" by 2 ¾" by 6". Nice!

Winning Bid: **$102.**^51

Ended: 1/16/04
History: 21 bids
Starting Bid: $9.99
Winner: California

Viewed
000304 X

The Story

I was at a garage sale in the best part of the Coachella Valley. I won't be writing exactly where, as I don't want to ruin my eBay business. My brother always warns me that if I talk about how great the sales are in certain areas, they will become overrun with eBayers. So I will bite my tongue.

I often find items that I need for myself or my house when I am out garage saling. I love it when I get great deals on these items, and that's what happened at this sale. The woman running the sale had incredible taste and was selling super-expensive items for next to nothing because she was moving. I found a gorgeous huge French ornate mirror for only $25 that I knew would look incredible over the faux fireplace in my living room. I quickly told the woman I would take it and continued to look around.

Next I saw a pair of Chanel sunglasses that were priced at only $15. I figured I could probably get $40 for them on eBay, and the profit from that sale would pay for my mirror. I bought both items and then spent 30 minutes struggling (unsuccessfully) to get the mirror into my BMW. Help! Luckily, my mother had moved down with her minivan. She wasn't around that Saturday, but on Monday morning we went together to pick up the mirror. I will never have to buy a truck or minivan now that my mom lives here! Life is good.

I put the sunglasses on eBay and immediately had several requests for confirmation that the glasses were authentic. The fact that they had the correct style number, were made in Italy, and came with the original box went a long way toward making people comfortable enough to bid top dollar. The sunglasses got 21 bids and brought in $102.51—far more than my original estimate. I made enough to buy 3 ½ mirrors! The man who won this auction had been searching for just that style to replace some glasses that his wife had lost.

The best part of this story came when I tried to hang that enormous mirror in my house. My dad was in town so I asked him to help me hang it, but it was just too cumbersome for us. I waited until my brother came to visit to try again, at which point my dad decided to "help" some more. My dad likes to be in charge—maybe that is what happens when you grow up with twelve siblings. Anyway, when he saw us wrestling with that mirror he started directing us, "Don't do it that way! Do it this way! It's crooked!" That was his way of helping. My brother and I were cracking up and rolling our eyes. We finally told him to leave the room, and we managed just fine without him. Yikes!

#23 Cat Pendants

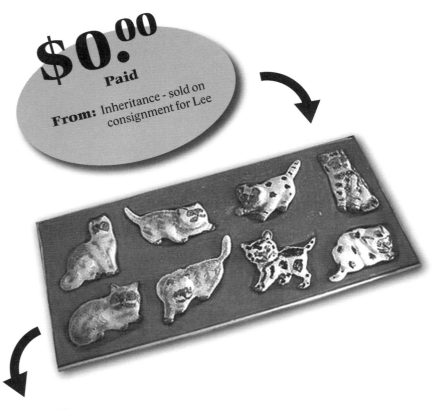

$0.00 Paid

From: Inheritance - sold on consignment for Lee

Peking Cat Enamel Jewelry-8 Pendants-Old-CUTE

Description:
This is a box of Peking jewelry that my grandmother brought back from the Orient in the 1980's. There are 8 vintage enamel-on-brass cat pendants in their original box. The pendants are in pretty good shape; a few have some green patina (which may clean up) and some enamel wear. The box is 8 ¼" by 3 ½".

Winning Bid: **$33.¹⁰**

Viewed
000089 X

Ended: 1/23/04
History: 11 bids
Starting Bid: $2.99
Winner: Washington

The Story

It was July 1979, and I was sitting on the floor in my grandmother's living room. It was the summer between my sophomore and junior year of high school and I was, as usual, working six days a week with my grandma. We were pricing books, and one of the books was a travel guide to the Orient. When she picked it up, she said, "I've always wanted to go to Hong Kong. It is one country I haven't visited yet."

My grandmother loved to travel and she went on trips often. Many summers she would let me run the shop and off she would go around the world. What an incredible experience for me as a young high school and college student—to be in charge of a business for two months!

This time was different. She looked at me and said, "How would you like to go to Hong Kong?" "Sure," I replied. I am always up for an adventure. Then she said, "Do you think your brother would like to go with us?" "Of course," I said. She stood up, got her travel agent on the phone and within 30 minutes we had tickets to Hong Kong leaving in two weeks. Back then, it was mandatory to have two weeks notice when making travel plans. If my grandmother had been making those plans today, we would probably have taken off the next morning! My grandmother never let the grass grow under her feet!

We spent two weeks in Hong Kong and a day in China. What an experience. She gave us each $200 to spend on clothes. That was a lot of money then! My brother and I had the best time racing from shop to shop. My grandmother was in her element. She met a delightful merchant on that trip named Mr. Wong,

and she spent a lot of money with him. Over the years, he sold her enough wonderful treasures to fill many containers. Hong Kong became one of my grandmother's favorite places to get items for the shop; she ended up going back at least ten times. Mr. Wong became a family friend and sometimes my grandmother would stay with his family instead of in a hotel.

On that first trip, my grandmother picked up twenty sets of these enamel cat pendants. She probably paid less than a dollar per set. Fast-forward 25 years and my brother gets a set with his inheritance and asks me to sell it for him. Boy, did it bring back memories—I had fun going through the old photo albums looking for the perfect "vintage" photo of us from that trip. I put the cats on eBay starting at $9.99 and no one bid. I lowered the price to $2.99, and if you can believe it, they got eleven bids and ended up selling for $33.10!

#24 Pink Guilloche Stopper

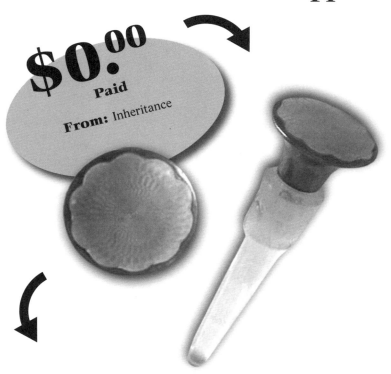

$0.00 Paid

From: Inheritance

SILVER French Pink Guilloche Perfume Stopper!

Description:
This stopper was in my grandmother's personal guilloche collection. She had many amazing pieces and often put parts away waiting for the perfect match. This is a pink guilloche French enamel stopper; the top is marked "sterling," and the base is glass. 1890's to 1920's or so. It will look great in that perfume bottle that is missing a stopper. It is 3 ⅛" long and 1 ⅛" in diameter at the top. The ground portion of the stopper goes from ⅝" to almost ¾". In excellent condition—a lovely piece.

Winning Bid:

$49.⁹⁹

Ended: 1/29/04
History: 1 bid
Starting Bid: $49.99
Winner: Colorado

Viewed
000096 X

Pink Guilloche Stopper   #24

The Story

I was getting ready to go on my first real scuba diving trip since becoming certified in the fall of 2003. My friend Peter and I were going to the Bahamas for a week. I was pretty nervous, so in order to avoid thinking too much about diving, I tried to focus on writing up a ton of auctions to run in my absence.

My average ticket price on eBay varies between $15 and $20, and I would like it to be a lot higher. I am constantly working on this, and I wanted to sell more expensive items while I was out of town so that my income wouldn't suffer. To make this happen, I needed to dig through some of my grandmother's personal items.

I found this beautiful pink perfume stopper in with some of her things. It was sterling, in a French style called "guilloche" that my grandmother collected. Guilloche is a type of enameling in which translucent enamel or fused glass is applied over a metal surface that has been engraved. This type of engraving is done with thin lines interwoven to create a patterned surface in a geometric design—very intricate and beautiful.

When I was little, the cabinet that housed her guilloche collection was one of my favorites. I loved it when she unlocked it and let me poke my little head in and browse. I can still remember the antique smell of the cabinet. I kept quite a few pieces of guilloche for myself, but this was just an orphaned stopper. I thought it would bring $50 to $100, so I decided to sell it to finance my trip. My grandmother would have approved. Travel was always a priority for her.

The Bahamas trip was a huge boost to my self-confidence. The first day out on the boat was incredibly stormy, and I said to Peter, "I am NOT going in." The dive master said, "You will get sick if you stay on top. You will feel much better underneath where the water is calm." I took a deep breath—a very deep breath—and jumped in. I am still a big scaredy cat and my eyes get huge when I am under water. My eyes are very blue and when they get as big as saucers they can alarm people. Dive masters are always asking me, "Are you OK?"

Luckily, I survived all four of my dives—even the very last one, where Peter got us lost and I could have killed him right there underwater as we looked for the boat. But we won't get into that story—there isn't enough room in this book.

I started the bidding on the stopper at $49.99. I had decided I would be happy to sell it for that price, but absolutely no less. It only got one bid, but that's all it took. I was pleased, and it helped to pay for my trip—and this goofy photo!

#25 White Wicker Chair

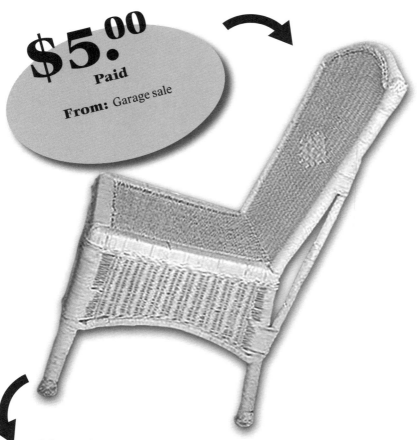

$5.⁰⁰ Paid

From: Garage sale

White Wicker Antique Chair-Great Vintage-WOW!

Description:
This is the best white wicker chair. It is vintage, in very good condition with only very minor damage. Dimensions are 37" tall, 20" deep and 16 ½" wide. It is painted a vintage glossy white. Very cool!

Winning Bid: **$76.⁵⁹**

Ended: 2/1/04
History: 4 bids
Starting Bid: $49.99
Winner: Tennessee

Viewed
 **X**

White Wicker Chair   #25

The Story

I had sent out review copies of *The 100 Best Things* to every major bookstore and television show, and I was just waiting to be flooded with orders and offers. Guess what? Nothing happened. The phones were silent. This was far different from my previous experiences writing books. What was up?

When my brother and I self-published a book about Beanie Babies in 1997, guess who bankrolled us? Cheryl Leaf. She asked how much we needed, and we told her $25,000. Without batting an eye, she said "Let's take it out of my Vanguard Fund." After *The Book of Beanie Babies* was printed, we sent it off, and within a week had huge orders from Waldenbooks, Borders, and Barnes & Noble. We also got a phone call from Scholastic.

I still remember standing in the antiques store when that call came in. I kept mouthing to my grandma and dad, "You won't believe this phone call . . . .You won't believe this phone call." I hung up and started screaming. Scholastic had offered my brother and I $50,000 to write *The Unauthorized Beanie Baby Guide!*

But that was back in 1997. With my new book it seemed that times had changed. What to do now? There was no Cheryl Leaf around to bail me out, and I needed to pay my printer quite a bit of money for those first 4,000 copies. Oh, how I miss my grandmother—in more ways than one! I realized I had better start putting a lot more stuff on eBay. I found this wicker chair at a garage sale for only $5, so I bought it.

Mari, my assistant, was always upset when I brought home big items. She had even got to the point where she would say, "I guess you will be packing this one" when I hauled in a large item. Antique and vintage wicker pieces can sell for quite a bit, so I was excited to try this darling chair despite Mari's packing boycott.

Wicker is a general term used for items woven from natural materials such as willow, reed and rattan. Authentic antique wicker pieces were made in the time period from 1870 to 1930. If you can believe it, this country went wicker crazy back then, and anything you can imagine was made from wicker: lamps, chairs, footstools, plant stands, bookshelves, desks, tea carts, and even music stands!

I didn't think my chair was from the authentic "Wicker Period," so I just called it vintage. "Vintage" is a very broad term, and I use it for anything from the 1940's to the 1990's. I was pleasantly surprised when my chair sold for over $75! I charged $35 UPS shipping, handling and insurance and off I went to pack it. I had to make a box that outlined the shape of the chair so it wouldn't exceed UPS's maximum allowable size. It was a lot of work! I haven't hauled any chairs home in a while, but I do keep self-publishing books. Will I ever learn?

#26 Box of Dentalium

$0.⁰⁰ Paid

From: Inheritance

Box Antique Dentalium Native American-Vintage

Description:
Box full of antique/vintage dentalium. They measure 1" to 1 ⅞" long. Great for jewelry making. Originally used by Native Americans as a form of money. My grandmother had these put away for many years. In great shape. There are anywhere from 50 to 100 pieces—I did not count them.

Winning Bid:

$32.⁹⁹

Ended: 2/3/04
History: 9
Starting Bid: $9.99
Winner: Alaska

Viewed
000110 X

Box of Dentalium #26

The Story

My grandma grew up in the Wenatchee valley in eastern Washington State in a tiny town called Cashmere. I loved to hear stories from her childhood. I sometimes thought that if we had been in school together, we would have been best friends; in fact, even with the 50-plus years between us, she *was* my best friend. She loved life and believed everything was an adventure. She always had a smile on her face.

When she passed away, the letters and pictures started pouring in from her closest childhood friends. It was amazing. Her dear friend Ruth Long said, "Your grandmother was the life of the party and our ringleader." The funny thing was that my grandma didn't fit the typical "party girl" mold; she never drank, smoked, or tried drugs. She used to say she was "high on life."

I made a collage of pictures from my grandmother's days in Cashmere to display at her funeral in August of 2000: my grandma sitting on a friend's motorcycle, pretending to play a banjo, and swimming in the Wenatchee river. Those days seem idyllic to me and I often wonder how it must have been to live during a time that was in some ways so much simpler.

There were a lot of Native Americans in Eastern Washington. In fact, many of the towns in Washington State are named for Indian nations such as the Salishan, Wenatchee, and Toppenish. My grandmother always found the Native Americans captivating.

She used to stand in awe of the Indian chiefs when they would come into her father's bank with strands and strands of beads around their necks. My grandmother's love for beads began in the Wenatchee valley, and that fascination followed her throughout her life. She was a sucker for beads, and spent all her discretionary money on them. Never clothes for my grandmother—just more and more beads!

I found ten little boxes of dentalium tucked away in one of the boxes I inherited. I knew what it was because I had spent many hours listening and learning from my grandmother. She had told me that dentalium is a natural tubular shell found on the west coast that was used for trade in early times. When dentalium was strung into strands, it was known as wampum, and was used by some American Indians as money.

These dentalium beads were beautiful and quite large. I put them on eBay and over 100 people viewed my auction. The little box full sold for $32.99 and went to Alaska. I think my grandmother would have been very happy to know that they sold for so much! And I was happy to know I had nine more boxes just like it.

#27 Southwest Plane Ticket

$0.^{00} **Paid**

From: Frequent flier miles

Southwest Airlines Rapid Rewards R/T Voucher+
New Ticketless Travel—Good through Jan 2005!

Description:

You are bidding on 12 drink coupons. As a bonus, you will receive a FREE Southwest Airlines PAPERLESS Rapid Reward good for one free round-trip flight or two one-way flights anywhere Southwest flies to, in the continental U.S. Voucher expires 1/13/05. This Rapid Rewards voucher is the new paperless format. The benefits are the same as the old with one main exception: I must reserve the flight in your name. I'll email you the confirmation number after payment.

Winning Bid: $300.^{03}

Ended: 2/10/04
History: 11 bids
Starting Bid: $9.99
Winner: Mississippi

Viewed

000170 **X**

Southwest Plane Ticket #27

The Story

This is a heartwarming story (and it isn't all about me!). I have a ton of frequent flyer miles from using my American Express card. I charge everything on this card because it is due in full at the end of the month. It keeps me honest. Anyway, I found out that I could use 20,000 of my American Express miles to get a round-trip Southwest Airlines voucher. I had heard of people selling these on eBay and I thought I would give it a try.

There are a lot of regulations on eBay for selling travel-related items, and they change constantly. I always start with "eBay Help" if I'm considering auctioning an item I have questions about. At the time I was planning this auction, I discovered I couldn't sell the actual vouchers—but I could sell the drink coupons and then give the vouchers as a gift with purchase. So that's exactly what I did.

For no outlay of capital, it was pretty fun to turn some unwanted miles into over $300! The best part of this transaction was the buyer and his story. Cliff and his wife Debbie were married on March 17th, 1979. They are both teachers, and because they both needed to pursue their careers and their passion for helping others, they were living apart. Cliff was in Mississippi, teaching sports administration at the University of Southern Mississippi, and Debbie was in Texas teaching special education. In order to renew their wedding vows for their 25th wedding anniversary, Cliff needed a plane ticket that was easy to use. He knew that with a Southwest Airlines Rapid Reward he could change his reservation at the last minute and usually always get a seat. His schedule was changing on a daily basis and it was very important for him to get back to Amarillo on the day of his anniversary. That is why he bought the ticket from me on eBay.

Here is a part of the email he sent me: "Lynn, you played a very important part in a couple that loves one another very much, getting married once again after 25 wonderful years." What a heartwarming story! As an ending note, Cliff mentioned that while he and Debbie were planning their wedding, neither had thought about the fact that it fell on St. Patrick's Day. Cliff says he is grateful for this coincidence, explaining, "Now, when everyone is wearing green, I know it's time to go out and buy an anniversary card. That way, I can stay out of trouble. Good idea, huh?" You never know what story may be behind the item you are buying or selling on eBay. That is why eBay is such a fun a place—for everybody!

#28 Tibetan Puzzle Ring

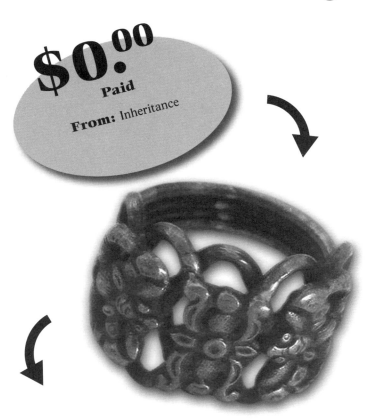

$0.⁰⁰ Paid

From: Inheritance

Puzzle Ring-Silver-Tibetan-Size 8-Antique-WOW

Description:

Puzzle ring is antique. I think it is from Tibet. Size 8. The top portion is ⅞" by ⅝". Very unusual, ornate top—in excellent shape—not sterling. Very neat. Don't take it apart—you won't get it back together!

Winning Bid:

$57.⁵³

Ended: 2/13/04
History: 14 bids
Starting Bid: $9.99
Winner: Japan

Viewed
000119 X

Tibetan Puzzle Ring #28

The Story

At age eighteen I moved, all by myself, from Bellingham (very small town) to Los Angeles (very huge town) to start college at USC. This still freaks me out, and I tell the story every time we pass the hotel where the airport shuttle first dropped me off in LA. My kids are sick of hearing about it and have started saying, "Mommy, we know, we know! You moved to LA all by yourself, blah, blah, blah."

I can't believe my parents and my grandmother just let me go off alone like that. But that was a different time. I know my kids won't be following my example!

Anyway, I arrived in LA with two suitcases and managed to find my way to campus. The realization soon sunk in that I was not in Kansas anymore. One of the first girls I met was Annie Hurtado. She was hysterically funny and drove a brand new red BMW. I, on the other hand, had left my green 1964 Volkswagen Beetle in Bellingham.

Annie and I became fast friends, then sorority sisters, and are still great friends to this day. She and her kids were coming from New Jersey to San Diego for the weekend, so I decided to take my kids and join them at Sea World. I would be missing my usual Saturday morning garage sales, so I started digging through boxes from my grandmother and I found this puzzle ring.

My grandmother had told me what type of ring it was, and I thought I remembered it was from Tibet. A puzzle ring consists of several interconnected rings that can be aligned as a finger ring. When the rings are taken apart,

it is almost impossible to believe that they ever made a single ring, and it's even harder to put back together.

I thought it was a really neat piece, and my first step in writing up the auction was to measure it with my grandmother's old ring mandrel (a conical tool used to determine ring size). Rings sell better when you're able to list their size. If you want to sell a ring and you don't have a ring mandrel—and I'm sure most of you do not—then stop by a local jewelry store and ask them to do the measuring for you.

The ring sold for a lot of money ($57.53) while I was in San Diego having fun with Annie and her family. It is amazing that we both survived college and actually have children. I have known Annie's family for a long time and her dad used to sarcastically call us "the spinsters." He joked that we would both end up unmarried with a bunch of cats. Strange thing is, I am currently unmarried and still have the cat I got with my ex-husband 15 years ago. That cat is my nemesis. Funny how life works—Annie's dad was right about me (in a strange kind of way).

#29 Tony the Tiger

$5.^{00}
Paid
From: Garage sale

Tony the Tiger Large Inflatable Toy-Kellogg's!

Description:
We have other Kellogg's promo stuff up for auction this week. This is a super cute Tony the Tiger large inflatable toy in orange, black and white. He is so cool! He will be about 4 feet tall when inflated and the package is 14" by 14". Mint in the original package.

Winning Bid:

$31.^{00}

Ended: 2/14/04
History: 3 bids
Starting Bid: $9.99
Winner: Japan

Viewed
 X

The Story

I was sitting at my desk one day putting things on eBay when I noticed I had mail. I was glad for any excuse to take a little break from the monotony of listing. Yes, I really did say that. It is true: eBay can get monotonous, and everybody who does eBay regularly knows it. I am just brave enough to put it in writing. I clicked over to my inbox and saw that I'd received a note from Dennis Prince.

Dennis Prince has written a lot of books about eBay. When I started trying to learn about online auctions in 1998, I bought every eBay book Amazon had—all four or five of them. Now, if you search on Amazon for a how-to book about eBay, you'll find over 300! Anyway, I read Dennis' book and really enjoyed it. When I developed my tracking books *i sell* and *i buy,* I sent copies to him to get his feedback. He was very nice and offered some good suggestions. We emailed back and forth a few times and then I didn't hear from him until that email in 2004—almost five years later!

He said he was working on a series of eBay books and was looking for an antiques expert to co-author a book with him and he thought of me. To make a long story short, he and I wrote a proposal and ended up getting a nice contract with McGraw Hill. Let the games begin.

I hadn't written a book for anyone other than Scholastic (and myself), and boy was it a different experience. Scholastic changed virtually none of what we wrote; they let my brother and I go wild. Donya Dickerson, my editor at McGraw, actually did some editing. The first few chapters I sent her came back drastically revised, and a lot of the personal details I had included—such as stories about my grandmother—were thrown out. It was going to be a wild ride!

All the while this was going on, I had to continue to list 100 new items each week to pay the bills. I found this plastic Tony the Tiger for $5 at the garage sale of a former Kellogg's sales rep. Tony was inflatable and really cute. I think that if I had inflated him, I might have been able to take a better picture (and ended up with a better sales price). However, the fact that I left him in his original package may have been more important. You just never know!

Tony sold on Valentine's Day to a woman in Japan. American promotional products tend to sell very well over there, and this item was just kitschy enough to garner attention (and bids) from several Japanese eBayers. The winning bidder even paid $17 to ship it airmail. Don't overlook the international market when selling on eBay. Some sellers will only ship domestically, and this really hurts their business. Just notice how many items in this book have gone overseas— even one of the most expensive ones (check out the Baccarat Chandelier, #57). "Sell globally and buy locally" —how's that for a slogan?

#30 Babe Ruth Figurine

$15.⁰⁰
Paid
From: Garage sale

Babe Ruth Danbury Mint Statue-Baseball-MIB!

Description:

We have 1 football and 7 baseball figurines/statues up for auction this week. This figurine is from the Danbury Mint Cooperstown Collection Baseball Legends. All Star Figurines. All come mint in the original boxes and are vintage 1998, 1999. They are in great shape but could use a good cleaning. They come with a beautiful wood base and brass name plate. This auction is for Babe Ruth New York Yankees Statue.

Winning Bid: **$100.⁰⁰**

Ended: 2/16/04
History: 9 bids
Starting Bid: $9.99
Winner: Texas

Viewed
000173 X

Babe Ruth Figurine   #30

The Story

I had baseball on the brain. My son, Houston, was deep into the spring baseball season. He was turning into an amazing little player. Houston's grandfather and father both loved baseball and had been good athletes, so Houston came by it naturally. In fact, Houston's great-grandfather on his dad's side, one-time mayor of Perth Amboy, N.J., even met Babe Ruth. We have a picture of him with the Babe. Now that is cool!

Anyway, my mom and I came upon a garage sale with a ton of collectibles—items such as collector's plates and figurines that were all the rage in the 1970's. I am all too familiar with this type of item; my grandmother went nuts with them when they were really popular and made a ton of money. The market just isn't the same as it was thirty years ago. Collecting is cyclical, just like everything else.

On one table were eight sports figurines by Danbury Mint, mostly baseball players, priced at $25 each. Way too expensive! I asked the woman holding the sale what she would take for all of them. (I always ask for a volume discount—believe me, it works!) She said she would not go any less than $15 each because she knew that they would sell for a lot on eBay.

Don't you just cringe when a seller says that? If someone has gone to the trouble of looking something up on eBay before pricing it, I can be pretty sure I won't be getting a bargain. The way this garage sale was run, however, suggested that this lady wasn't really very knowledgeable about collectibles or eBay. It seemed that there might be some wiggle room here.

So I told her "Fine, I will take them for $120." I started them all on eBay at $9.99 each. I had done my research,

and the Babe was the best one. The most he had sold for in the last month was $61.69. I made sure to note in my listing that I had others in the series up for sale. This is a surefire way to get more bids! Always list like items at the same time.

The Babe ended up selling for $100! The fact that it was baseball season may have helped push up the price. Altogether, the eight pieces sold for $487.33. I grossed $367.33 before my eBay and PayPal fees. Not baggy (as my mom would say). I have no idea why she says that. However, I digress.

I have come to the conclusion that I would rather double, triple or quadruple my money on eight easy items than make ten times on forty $1 items. You see how that works—I made $367 with only handling eight items. If I was doing my usual "make ten times" rule and bought 40 items at $1 each and they all sell for $10 each—I have made $360 also but I have had to handle 40 things! I am getting smarter!

#31 10 Silver & 10 Gold Prisms

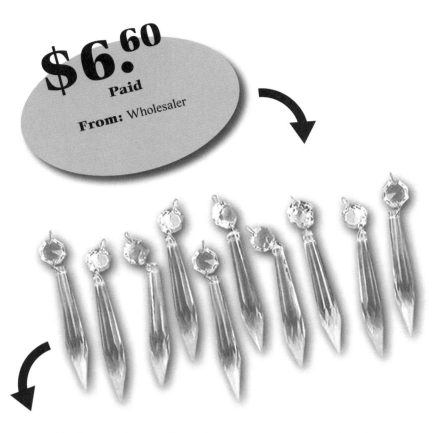

$6.⁶⁰ **Paid**

From: Wholesaler

10 Crystal Czech Prisms 4" NEW-Lovely-Silver!

Description:

10 beautiful "Made in Czech" crystal glass prisms. They are 4" from the top button to the base with silver colored metal for accent. These are great for lamps, chandeliers and for ornaments on a Christmas tree. In perfect brand new condition.

Winning Bid:

$57.⁰⁰ /2

Ended: 3/1/04
History: 13 bids/2
Starting Bid: $4.99
Winner: Missouri

Viewed
 X

10 Silver & 10 Gold Prisms   #31

The Story

My grandmother always carried lamp parts such as replacement chimneys, burners, prisms, and wicks in her store. It was a very savvy move, because having the best selection of specialty lamp parts in town brought in foot traffic. Once the customers were inside, they would usually buy something else–making a great add-on sale.

Having an eBay store is basically just a way of selling things on eBay at a fixed price rather than in an auction. When I first heard about eBay stores, I was intimidated. I thought opening one would involve setting up a big huge web site, so I put it off for quite a while.

When I finally got around to starting an eBay store, I found that it was simple! All I had to do was pay eBay a certain monthly fee (of course) and then just move any item that didn't sell at auction into the store by selecting the "Sell at a Fixed Price in my store" button. The first items I listed were these new crystal glass prisms, following my grandma's example by putting high-demand items into my store to drive in traffic. She was a successful businesswoman, and I am doing my best to emulate her.

She and I were both nominated for Whatcom County Business Woman of the year—my grandma in 1991 and I in 2001. Neither of us won, but it was an honor just to be considered. I owe so much of my business success to my

The Bellingham Herald
October 13, 1991

Cheryl Leaf

Whatcom County Businesswoman of the Year Award

Cheryl Leaf
Cheryl Leaf Antiques and Gifts

Whatcom County Business Pulse   October 2001

Lynn Wilson

Professional Woman of the Year Award

grandma—don't they say that "imitation is the sincerest form of flattery"?

I now list 50 prisms in both gold and silver metal in my eBay store for 99 cents each. I also list ten of each every week at a cheaper price using the auction format. My goal in doing this is to drive traffic to my store. It's a different kind of "traffic," but it's the same principle that worked for my grandmother. Boy, hasn't the world changed in the past ten years?

Anyway, here is why this story is so amazing. I started the auctions for each set of prisms at $4.99 (half of what they are priced in my eBay store). On this particular week, I got several bidders who had not done their research before going crazy. The same woman won both auctions. She paid $26 for ten gold prisms and $31 for ten silver prisms, for a total of $57! If she had done her due diligence and looked in my eBay store, she could have bought all twenty for $19.80.

I have to admit that when this happens, it makes me feel bad. I don't like to take advantage of anyone, but as they say, "Let the buyer beware." And it wasn't just the winning bidder who got auction fever—the other eBay bidder clearly had it, too! Amazing! Bidding frenzies make eBay such a fun place to do business.

#32 Staffordshire Dog

$0.⁵⁰ Paid

From: Garage sale

Lancaster & Sons Staffordshire Spaniel Dog-Antique-NICE

Description:
Signed "L & Sons Ltd. Made in England," Staffordshire Spaniel Dog. The "L & Sons" stands for Lancaster & Sons, who were in business in Stoke on Trent from 1900-1944. This darling dog is Staffordshire; color is cream with yellow and black painted details. He has overall crazing (quite normal/typical) and there is a flake chip on the back side near the base which measures ⅜" by ⅜". There is also a tiny tiny speck of black paint missing. These dogs have been popular since Victorian times.

Winning Bid: **$37.⁶⁷**

Ended: 3/9/04
History: 5 bids
Starting Bid: $9.99
Winner: Tennessee

Viewed
 X

Staffordshire Dog #32

The Story

There was actually going to be a garage sale in my gated community. How exciting! I wouldn't have to get up at 6:00 AM that Saturday. I could actually sleep in until 6:30! Getting up early on Saturdays is the absolute worst part of my job. I am NOT a morning person. I keep hoping someone will organize a Thursday evening garage sale extravaganza here, as I have heard they do elsewhere. But no! Too many old-timers here like their garage sales to start early.

My mom and I arrived to the sale right on time, and I bought a white dinner set and this little dog. I could tell he was Staffordshire, but I didn't know how old he was. He was only priced at 50 cents, so why not? I remembered many spaniel dogs like this over the years from my grandmother's store.

I got the dog home and did some research. He was signed "L & Sons Ltd." I Googled it and found that "L & Sons" was actually Lancaster & Sons, which was only in business from 1900 to 1944. Score! That made him easy to date.

He would originally have had a matching left-facing dog and would probably have been placed on a fireplace mantel. These matching dog figurines were very popular in Victorian times and are still quite collectible. Intact pairs of spaniels dating from the 1860's to 1880's can fetch $500 to $1,000. Since mine wasn't that old and was missing his buddy, I knew he wasn't going to sell for a whole lot. But what did I have to lose? I had paid only 50 cents.

When I went to list him, I was astonished to see that eBay let me run on and on with my title. eBay had always limited titles to 45 characters, and all of a sudden I was allowed to go to 55! Since I was writing the book with Dennis Prince, I immediately emailed him to see if he had noticed. He hadn't. There was no announcement from eBay either—just a quiet change on the "Sell your item" form. But this was HUGE! Ten extra characters meant space for words like "Victorian," "Collectible" and "Antique" that I used to have to sacrifice for other more important search terms.

I put the spaniel on eBay with the new, longer title. How exciting! He sold for $37.67 and went to Tennessee. What a great return on four bits. I still remember when I first learned what "four bits" was. I was six years old and at a garage sale with my mom. She asked the woman running the sale, "How much for this game?" "Four bits," was the answer. "What?" I asked my mom. It was the strangest thing I had ever heard. She taught me to count, "Two bits, four bits, six bits, a dollar," so I learned that four bits was 50 cents. I still can't believe I remembered this—and just when I needed an ending to this story.

#33 Seal Jumbo Press

$10.00 Paid

From: Garage sale

Seal Jumbo 160 Dry Mount Laminating/Laminator Press NR

Description:

This is a Seal Jumbo 160 Dry Mounting Laminating Press. It is vintage and very heavy (about 50 pounds). It is rusty as you can see in the photos. This should not affect its performance. This tabletop unit is heat-activated and is a dry mount press used by photographers for mounting and flattening photos. This is a simple, easy-to-use tool.

Winning Bid: **$152.50**

Ended: 3/9/04
History: 9 bids
Starting Bid: $9.99
Winner: New York

Viewed

 **X**

Seal Jumbo Press #33

The Story

My dad was in town to celebrate his 70th birthday with two of his kids (me and Lee) and two of his grandkids (Houston and Indy). Your 70th birthday should always be something spectacular. I didn't consider spending the week in Palm Desert "spectacular," so I tried to get my dad to do something crazy. I offered to pay for him to go up in a hot air balloon. "No, no, no," he said. He is so conservative, both with his money and with his lifestyle. I worked on him for about an hour and then gave up. Life is too short—both for him and for me. So instead of hot-air ballooning, we all went to the Outback for steak. Whoooppppeee!

When my dad turned 60, I took out an advertisement in our local newspaper, *The Bellingham Herald*. I put a caption saying "Happy 60th Birthday! Wayne Dralle" around a photo of him when he was a kid. Everyone in town called him—he was so mad! I knew I had better not do that again. There are only about two known photos of my father as a child, but they prove that he was really cute! He came from a hard-working South Dakota farming family with thirteen kids. I think he picked up his conservative attitude in that environment. One thing I did not learn from my dad was to be conservative. I like to live every day like it is my last. I take risks on a daily basis—especially with my eBay business.

I dragged my dad out with me to some garage sales on a Friday morning when the kids were at school. We were leaving one when my dad found something interesting on the ground. It was an old press that would probably have been used by a photographer. My dad was always into photography and now my brother is a professional photographer.

They wanted $10 for it, and it was really heavy. I asked my dad whether he thought I should buy it, and of course he wouldn't commit to anything. So, based on his hemming and hawing (which was more on the positive side than normal), I decided to take a chance. Good thing! My brother helped me write the description (those are definitely not my words)! It ended up selling for over $150 to a buyer in New York. The winning bidder even paid $40 for shipping. That was the high point of my dad's 70th birthday for me!

#34 Gorham Flatware Set

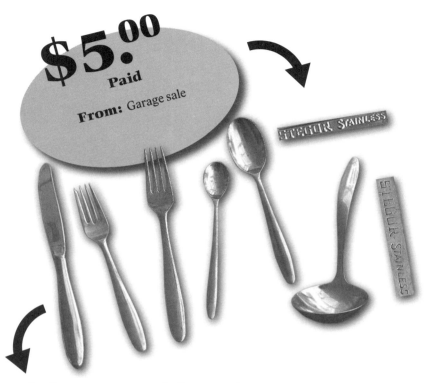

$5.00 Paid

From: Garage sale

STEGOR STAINLESS

STEGOR STAINLESS

Gorham Stegor Stainless 6 Dinner Knives-Pace-Modern

Description:

We have quite a few pieces in this pattern up for auction this week. All are just signed "Stegor Stainless," except for the iced tea spoons which are signed "Gorham." I am guessing that this is the Pace pattern. This is really neat with a nice sleek shape that looks Eames-era Danish mod. This auction is for 6 stainless dinner knives 9". They are not signed with anything but "stainless." All pieces are in very good shape with the usual estate slight wear.

Winning Bid:

$244.⁸⁰/8

Ended: 4/13/04
History: 41 bids/8
Starting Bid: $9.99 each
Winner: WA, MD, TX, WI

Viewed
000276 X

Gorham Flatware Set #34

The Story

This just goes to show you that eBay really is a numbers game and that you have to kiss a lot of frogs (or is it toads?) before you find your Prince Charming. Believe me, I have made my share of mistakes. I make them every week. It is all part of the learning and growing process. I figure that if I'm not making mistakes, then I must be dead.

I put 100 new items on eBay every single week, even if I'm writing a book, traveling for business, or on a vacation. I have had the 100-item goal for about eight years and I don't think I have missed more than four weeks—the four weeks it took to move all my stuff—and my computer! —from Bellingham, Washington, to Southern California.

By putting 100 new things on each week, I can guarantee a certain income level. It all averages out. Some things that I think will sell for hundreds of dollars don't, and other things that I think won't go for $3 end up selling for $50. This is why eBay is so much fun and the reason I make myself live up to that 100-item goal each week.

The beauty of eBay is that you are your own boss and you can make as much or as little money as you want or have time for. I was really sick the other day and I said to my daughter Indiana, "I had better call in sick today to my boss." She looked at me with a completely puzzled expression and said, "What is a boss?" Is that priceless from a seven-year-old? I am so lucky that I get to spend every day working from home with my two great kids in the next room.

Anyway, I was at a garage sale and saw a complete set of silverplated flatware for $25. I scooped it right up thinking it was going to be great on eBay. Next to it was a partial box of stainless steel flatware—twenty assorted pieces for $5. They were very sleek, mid-century modern and only 25 cents apiece, so I bought them.

Well, here is where my lesson takes place. I barely broke even on the silverplated set—I think some of it is still in my eBay store. The stainless, however, sold in eight separate auctions for $244.80! It was amazing. One of the buyers (Susie) emailed me to say, "When my parents got married in 1955 they chose this pattern for their flatware. I remember using it when I was a kid until my mother got rid of it in the 1970's and the original set was demoted to 'camping' gear. I rediscovered it in all its 'mid-century modern' glory and began hunting down pieces on eBay to round out my new set." What a great story!

What really blew my mind was that Susie paid $92 for the six dinner knives she bought. Yikes. The job perks with eBay never stop. Making money from home, spending time with my kids, and—oh yeah— "What's a boss?"

#35 Tiffany Sterling Pill Box

$5.00
Paid
From: House sale

Tiffany Sterling Pill-Trinket Box Basketweave DARLING!

Description:
Lovely box is signed "Tiffany & Co. Sterling Italy 925." Use as a pill box or trinket box. It needs polishing but is in excellent condition. There is a gold wash on the inside and some slight wear. Basketweave pattern. 1 ⅜" by ⅞" by ½"; box is not hinged.

Winning Bid:

$123.50

Ended: 4/14/04
History: 15 bids
Starting Bid: $9.99
Winner: Maryland

Viewed
 **X**

Tiffany Sterling Pill Box #35

The Story

My grandmother collected boxes—mainly patch boxes, but she loved anything with a hinge. She kept them in a coffee table with a glass top. She loved to pull out each box and describe it: the type of glass it was made of, its maker, where it was from, its age, and what it was worth. It was a wonderful way for us kids to learn about antiques.

The museum in Bellingham held a tea each year to showcase some of the more interesting local collections. My grandma exhibited several times and when she was invited in 1994, we decided to bring her box collection. My grandmother had a great time at that tea, catching up with friends, chatting, and talking about her boxes!

There was nothing my grandmother enjoyed more than socializing. One of the first questions she would ask a new friend was, "What do you collect?" What a great icebreaker. We all collect something, don't we? My grandmother knew that what a person collects reveals a great deal about them—and collectors are what make eBay the success that it is today.

I was out garage saling with my mom and we stumbled upon a doozy of an estate sale. The woman holding the sale was an incurable collector and was selling out, floor to ceiling. In one room, she had a display case that was completely filled with boxes. I couldn't believe it—the collection looked a lot like my grandmother's! There were about 60 boxes altogether, and she wanted $300 for them. Sold! I didn't have $300 with me, so we gave her a deposit and ran over to my bank. Big mistake, but I will tell you more about that later.

We returned with the money, paid, and started wrapping the boxes. Out of the corner of my eye I saw two antiques dealers I knew opening the kitchen cupboards. My heart sank. I hadn't even thought about looking through the kitchen. They pulled out three amazingly expensive china sets with numerous serving pieces. One was a blue chintz. Those pieces go for big bucks on eBay.

I was heartbroken, and followed the dealers as they went to negotiate a price. The seller wanted $600 for all of the sets. I would have paid it in a second, but they were trying to talk the price down. I waited, hoping they would decide to walk away. Unfortunately, the dealers ended up buying all the sets.

I couldn't stop thinking about overlooking those china sets. I have been kicking myself ever since. My grandmother never would have let something like that bother her, but I can't seem to forget it. I am hoping that writing about it here will be cathartic. On a better note, one of the little boxes that I paid $5 for was a Tiffany and sold for $123.50! I got over $900 for all the boxes and ended up making about $600. But I can't stop wondering how much I could have made on those dishes......

#36 Portmeirion Bowl

$10.⁰⁰
Paid
From: House sale

Portmeirion Big Bowl-Botanic Garden-Blue Passion Flower

Description:
Neat Portmeirion Large Serving Bowl is marked "1972 The Botanic Garden c 1818." It is 11 ¼" by 5 ¼". Susan Williams-Ellis, Made in England. In the center are blue passion flowers and butterflies. Around the sides are trailing bindweed, spring gentian, meadow saffron, daisy, ivy leaves, and cyclamen—NICE.

Winning Bid:

$84.⁰⁰
Ended: 4/15/04
History: 15 bids
Starting Bid: $9.99
Winner: Kentucky

Viewed
000122 X

Portmeirion Bowl #36

The Story

I was still at the same house sale and did not plan to leave until everything was sold. I was NOT going to miss another bonanza as I had with the china. I slowly walked around the house looking for anything that I might have missed. On the dining table was a bowl with fruit in it. The woman wanted $10 for it. It seemed like an awful lot and she wasn't even going to throw in the fruit. Just kidding—I didn't really want the fruit. Too many carbs.

I removed the fruit and turned the bowl over, looking for marks. I recognized the pattern and the maker's name, "Portmeirion Botanic Garden." When I had chosen my everyday wedding china in 1993, I had picked a Portmeirion pattern called "Welsh Dresser." It is similar to Botanic Garden, but not as popular. Portmeirion is expensive and very high quality, so I bought the bowl and walked out dejectedly.

"Oh, woe is me," I moaned. My mom was like, "Shut up already! So you missed the mother lode—there will be others!" I couldn't stop thinking about the 200-plus pieces of fine china I had just not bought. Still can't. Fishermen (especially my father) are known for talking incessantly about "the one that got away"–and now I think I understand! I am sorry that this sad tale had to weave its way through two of my stories. I promise that this is it. I am finished with this incident and will never speak of it again, so help me God.

Portmeirion was founded as a tableware company in the 1960's by Susan Williams-Ellis. She had been creating pottery works for her father's gift shop at the Portmeirion Village in North Wales for years when she and her husband Euan decided to buy two pottery companies in order to expand their product lines.

The company started out slowly, but in the early 1970's Susan accidentally came across a nineteenth-century book of prints, some of which she adapted into the Botanic Garden line of tableware. Botanic Garden has become one of the world's biggest-selling tableware patterns and still accounts for half of Portemeirion's sales. Wow!

Now this was exciting. I hadn't realized just how popular Botanic Garden was. I got on the Replacements.com web site to find the name and selling price of this bowl. I love this web site and use it for most of my tabletop research.

There are thousands of pieces and pattern combinations in this pattern, and my bowl turned out to be the large salad bowl in the Passion Flower sub-pattern. Replacements.com didn't have any in stock. Always a good sign! This hard-to-find item ended up selling for $84 to a buyer in Kentucky. It helped ease my pain—a little bit—over the fish that got away!

#37 Pair Alabaster Lamps

$5.00 Paid

From: Garage sale

Alabaster/Marble Vintage PAIR Table Lamps-Eames Era!!

Description:

Great pair of alabaster marble column table lamps. They are 4 ¼" square at the base. The marble portion is 16" tall. The entire lamp is 29 ½" tall. Vintage; I would guess 1920's to 1950's Eames-era classic. They are carved and have a very classic form. They need the perfect shades and rewiring. The finials don't match but the lamps do, and it is very very hard to find a matched pair! These are not perfect—they have some small chips and dings and some yellowing in the alabaster/marble, but for vintage, they are in very good shape.

Winning Bid:

$213.⁶¹

Ended: 4/15/04
History: 14 bids
Starting Bid: $9.99, $150 reserve
Winner: New York

Viewed

000288 X

Pair Alabaster Lamps #37

The Story

I learned at a very young age that antiques don't always sell for what they seem to be worth. Often, antique pieces (especially lamps, lighting, furniture and rugs) will be less expensive than similar items that are brand-new. My grandmother always told her customers, "Why don't you buy an antique to furnish your home? It will be cheaper than a new item, and the workmanship is far superior."

It never made any sense to my grandmother and me that a new lamp would sell for much more than a similar antique piece. A beautiful antique ceiling fixture in the shop might bring in $250, while a comparable brand new lamp, with no history and none of the same wonderful workmanship, might sell for $1,000. It always amazed us.

Whenever my grandmother traveled to an antiques show, I would usually pack. We always took a lot of table lamps, not only because they helped to light our booth, but also because they sold well to buyers looking to get a lot of value for their money. It took about 50 boxes full of antiques and collectibles to fill our booth. Scouting through the store picking which items to take always felt like going on a treasure hunt. I usually tried to select a broad variety of items. I was also responsible for packing all the extension cords, supplies, display cabinets—and the till.

My grandmother took the same metal till to every antiques show for 40 years. We kept our coin and dollar change inside, and checks went under the pull-out top portion. Today, this till sits in my office, and I use it to hold checks between trips to the bank.

Late one night when I was twelve, my grandmother and I were driving home from an antiques show. I was bored, and I loved math, so I decided to count all the change in the till. I added it up and asked my grandmother to guess the amount.

She started out slowly, saying "Thirteen dollars and . . . ." I couldn't believe it, but that was the dollar amount! Then she paused, finally coming out with "seventy-four cents." I freaked out. She had guessed the amount of money in the till to the penny (and no, she hadn't had time to secretly count it)! She whooped with laughter. We couldn't believe it, and we talked about the "till caper" for years.

I am always looking for lighting items. I spotted this pair of alabaster lamps for $5 at a garage sale. Definitely cheap enough. I did some research and found that they can sell in the $100 to $400 range—especially a matched pair. Alabaster is a type of streaky, translucent white or gray marble. It is often used for sculpture, clocks, mantel vases and lamps. I put the pair on eBay with a $9.99 starting bid and a reserve of $150. Even in their vintage condition, these sold for $213.61—almost exactly $200 over the amount that was in the till so many years ago.

#38 Vienna Bronze Inkwell

$0.⁰⁰ Paid

From: Kiki inherited

Vienna Bronze Bird/Chickadee Inkwell-Antique-Wonderful!

Description:
This wonderful piece comes from our grandmother's personal Vienna bronze collection. It is a chickadee or another type of bird. It is an 1880's antique and so amazing. Hinged lid with a shiny brass base as is typical of all bronze pieces. Originally painted and some of the paint remains. Marked near the tail with "Geschutz" (German for "registered" or "copyrighted"). It also has a "10" on it.

Winning Bid: **$860.⁰⁰**

Ended: 4/18/04
History: 11 bids
Starting Bid: $49, $499 Reserve
Winner: Pennsylvania

Viewed
 **X**

Vienna Bronze Inkwell #38

The Story

It was Easter week and I was back in Bellingham. It wasn't for a happy occasion. My really good girlfriend, Jodi Cadman Chalfant, had passed away, and I was in town for her funeral. Jodi had battled ovarian cancer for seven years. She fought like a champ and never complained. She was always smiling and concerned about what was going on in your life—not hers. She left behind her husband, Bob, and a 15-year-old daughter, Ashley.

When I was getting ready to move to LA, I was very sad about leaving my friends, family, and especially my grandmother. Jodi took the time to write me an amazing letter that I still have. She told me that although I was leaving a lot behind, it was the beginning of a new and exciting time in my life. She told me that I should be happy and thankful for the opportunity God was giving me. She was always so positive. I miss her.

The funeral was on Monday, so I flew up with my kids several days beforehand. My sister Kristin needed some money, so I offered to put twenty things on eBay for her. One of the items that I listed was this Vienna bronze. Vienna bronzes were all the rage, especially with the English, starting about 1850. They were manufactured in small factories in Vienna, Austria, and decorated with colorful paint. My grandmother had bought this bird in London in 1960.

Bronzes marked with "Geschutz" (meaning "copyright") are more valuable; luckily, this bird was marked. It was also particularly collectible because it was in the form of an inkwell, so I listed it in both the "Bronze" and "Inkwell" categories. I rarely list in two categories because it doubles the insertion fees for an auction. But this bronze was special—just like Jodi.

The auction started on Easter Sunday with a $49.99 starting bid price and a reserve of $499. As I was working at the computer, my family called me to the table. "Hold on," I said, "Just let me finish this one listing." I quickly pushed the "Submit" button and headed in for Easter dinner.

In Loving Memory

A time to weep, and a time to laugh; a time to mourn, and a time to dance...

An hour later, I headed back to the computer and was completely shocked to see that the bronze bird had already reached its reserve! What great news for my sister. The bird eventually sold for over $800.

The next day I had a funeral to attend. It turned out to be a wonderful celebration of Jodi's life, and the church was overflowing. Jodi's goal had been to live to turn 40. Can you imagine someone actually wanting to turn 40? She just barely made it. I will never complain about a birthday again. One of the songs Jodi chose, Leanne Womack's "I Hope You Dance," was her way of telling us all not to waste one single day. I hear that song a lot, and I always cry.

#39 Bakelite Pull Toy

$0.⁰⁰ **Paid**

From: Inheritance

754

Bakelite Pull Toy-Little Person Eames Era-Vintage 1950s

Description:
Darling little person (boy/girl) is 3 ¼" tall and 2 ¼" wide. Similar to a pull toy. He or she has a wooden hat and a wooden head. The rest of the body is made up of bakelite beads in red, gold and amber. Vintage 1950's era I would guess. In great condition.

Winning Bid:

$44.⁷⁵

Ended: 4/23/04
History: 9 bids
Starting Bid: $9.99
Winner: Maryland

Viewed

000104 X

Bakelite Pull Toy #39

The Story

Something great actually happened during that sad April month. My brother finally acquiesced and offered to sell me the boxes he had inherited from our grandmother. My constant inquiries (and Peter's great advice) had paid off. Lee was focusing on his photography business, and selling on eBay can be very time consuming. He was finally ready to let go and move on! Yippeee!

I agreed to pay for the U-Haul truck to get the boxes from LA to the desert. But where in the world was I going to put them? My garage, guest room and office were already crammed. But I wasn't afraid—I knew I would find a place. I think he had about 60 boxes left, and we agreed upon $50 a box. A bargain for me! It was also good for Lee, because he had been paying to store them in a storage unit and the monthly rental fees were eating into his potential profits.

Lee was three and I was six when our little sister was born. We have always gotten along really well. So, it was fun unloading the big U-Haul truck with him. I had spent a full day re-arranging my garage and there was finally space, so Lee and I carefully stacked all the boxes. I decided to go through them very slowly, but I couldn't wait to try just one box. It was so exciting—I couldn't resist. I found this little toy in that first box. What in the world was it?

The toy was marked with an old, old price sticker in my grandmother's handwriting that said "75 cents." The price tag was very small with two straight sides and two rounded sides. I am sure you are dying to know why, and I am going to tell you. My grandmother scrimped and saved and cut corners wherever she could. She knew that any money not spent on unnecessary extravagance went right to her bottom-line profit. She used to order the large-sized sticky price tags (the best value), and—if you can believe it—cut them into four smaller ones. This was one of her ¼ size price tags. The tags were so small that you could barely write on them.

I knew that this piece was definitely 1950's Eames era, but what could I call it so that people would find this auction? To be successful on eBay, you have to drive traffic to your auctions, and the title is your best chance of doing this. I saw that it was handmade from some bakelite beads. So bakelite would be a great angle. It also looked like those pull toys with arms and legs that move when a string is pulled. I put "bakelite," "pull toy," "Eames" and "vintage" in the title. I must have done a good job, because 104 people looked at this auction!

I was thrilled when this little toy sold for $44.75. Incredibly, it was almost enough to pay for the entire box of goodies I had bought from my brother. My grandmother would have gotten such a kick out of the fact that her 75-cent item had sold for $44 over what she had marked it. I wish I could tell her about it. But on some level, I think she already knows.

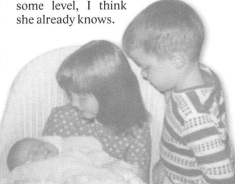

#40 Pan Am Vaseline Vase

$0.00 Paid
From: Inheritance

Pan American NY 1901 Vaseline Glass Vase-Rigoree-WOW!

Description:

Pan American 1901 vaseline glass vase. This vase has applied rigoree (ruffled glass décor) and is 103 years old. Look at the wonderful glow under a black light! 6 ¾" by 3 ¾". It does have a flake chip on one of the points. This is difficult to notice and hardly detracts from the beauty of the piece. There are also some water stains, as this vase was actually used. A wonderful piece from the Pan American Exposition in Buffalo, New York in 1901. It says "Pan American 1901" on the front in a medallion. There is also a circular medallion on the back.

Winning Bid:

$86.⁵⁵

Ended: 5/19/04
History: 8 bids
Starting Bid: $49.99
Winner: Boston, MA

Viewed

000157 X

Pan Am Vaseline Vase #40

The Story

It is January 25th as I write this story—my grandmother's birthday. She would have been 94 years old. My grandmother loved presents. She always found the perfect gift for everyone at each holiday, and she took great joy in receiving gifts, too.

When I lived in LA, I put a lot of energy into finding the perfect presents for her. I would wrap them carefully and ship them early to make sure they arrived on time. I always wrote on all sides of the box in big black pen, **"Do not open before 1/25."** I would call her on her birthday and say, "You didn't open the gifts early, did you?" And she would just laugh because she had torn them open the moment they arrived! She was terrible. She knew better, but she was just like a little kid, and I loved her all the more for it!

This vase was marked "1901." Amazing—my grandma and the vase were from the same era. My grandmother loved vaseline glass, which is made with 2% uranium dioxide; it glows green under an ultraviolet (black) light. My grandma's vaseline glass collection, which included this vase, was in her bedroom. When I moved back to Bellingham to run her store in 1993, she and I decided we should start to weed out some of the items from her personal collections, because she just had too much! This vase was one of the items that we decided should go.

We priced it at $125 and noted on the tag that it was being sold "as is." Any reputable seller, whether in a store or online, will note if something is chipped, cracked or crazed. "As is" covers everything and alerts a customer to ask, "What is wrong with this piece?" The listing for this item mentioned that it had a flake chip on one point and water stains inside.

This vase had not sold after seven years in the store, and it found its way to me in the first box I got from my brother. I thought it had a good chance of selling on eBay because Pan Am items are very collectible, as is vaseline glass.

The Pan American Exposition took place from May 1 to November 2, 1901, in Buffalo, New York, and featured such technological advances as electricity. On September 6, President McKinley was shot outside the Exposition's Temple of Music. He died eight days later, and on September 14, Theodore Roosevelt was inaugurated as president. Many people collect items from this exposition, which even has its own category number on eBay (#4165). I listed it in this category.

The vase ended up selling for $86.55, and we shipped it to New York State. From Buffalo, New York, to who knows where, to a shelf in my grandmother's bedroom, and then back to New York after 105 years. Strange, isn't it?

#41 Mideke Fertility God Statue

$0.⁰⁰ Paid

From: Inheritance

Louis Mideke Fertility God-Warrior Large Statue-Pottery

Description:

This is signed "MIDEKE" with a stamp on the lower portion. Louis Mideke was a very well known Washington State artist & potter. Some of his pieces are in the Smithsonian. This auction is for a warrior or fertility god; it is one of the last Mideke pieces that we have. Louis had a sense of humor as revealed by the face on the warrior's spear. Very rustic. In excellent condition but needs a cleaning. 14" by 4 ½" by 4 ½" and heavy. A great piece. 1960's or so.

Winning Bid:

$211.⁴⁹

Ended: 5/22/04
History: 3 bids
Starting Bid: $49.99
Winner: California

Viewed

000088 X

Mideke Fertility God Statue   #41

The Story

Louis Mideke was a very famous Washington State artist and potter. In fact, some of his pieces have been exhibited in the Smithsonian. Louis was well known for experimenting with the local clays and using natural resources in his glazes. Many people don't realize that he worked in many mediums—wood and metal, in addition to clay. He would never do what all the other potters of his time were doing; he forged his own way. This is why his pieces are so wonderful. He marched to the beat of his own drummer, just like my grandmother.

Louis's studio was in an old chicken coop behind his house off of Sunset Avenue in Bellingham, Washington. My grandmother's antiques store was at the bottom of Sunset Avenue. They became friends in the 1950's. My brother recently emailed me an article about Louis Mideke, and in it he was quoted as saying, "Don't run off mad." We got such a kick out of it, because my grandmother always used to say the same thing to us! We wonder who said it to whom first?

My grandmother always appreciated Louis's work and would stop by the chicken coop occasionally to pick up pieces to sell in her store. More often than not, she would keep them for her own collection. One of her favorite items to give us on birthdays and Christmas were pieces of his work. A few pieces from my Mideke collection are pictured—including a very rare metal lamp.

When Louis Mideke passed away in 1988, the contents of his home and studio were sold to the Good Earth Pottery in the Fairhaven section of Bellingham. In 1993, my grandmother and I bought everything that the Good Earth Pottery was unable to sell, about 200 pieces. It was a lot of fun.

Over the next ten years, most of the Mideke pieces sold. This big warrior or fertility god (as I called him) did not sell, and it showed up in a box that I inherited. He had been marked "LM524" and "$125" in our store. The "LM524" was the way the items were tagged by the Good Earth Pottery after he passed away. "LM" stood for Louis Mideke, as opposed to "JM," which stood for Jean, his wife, who was also an artist. "524" meant that it was the 524th item that they catalogued.

I thought this piece was really neat and put it on eBay with a starting price of $49.99; it sold for $211.49. I was so pleased to find that there are other Mideke aficionados out in the eBay world.

#42 Blue Calico Pitcher

$2.00 Paid
From: Garage sale

Blue Calico Chintz Staffordshire Large Pitcher/Milk Jug

Description:

Blue Calico Chintz Staffordshire Large Pitcher/Milk Jug is marked
"Crownford China Co. Inc. Staffordshire England." This is a large
pitcher (7 ½" by 6 ¾") in excellent condition. No chips, no cracks.

Winning Bid:

$78.10

Ended: 5/27/04
History: 10 bids
Starting Bid: $9.99
Winner: Florida

Viewed
 X

Blue Calico Pitcher #42

The Story

It was May and I was realizing that I was going to have to do more than just send my *100 Best* book out to store buyers. So far, Barnes & Noble was the only major bookstore that had agreed to carry it. This was very exciting, but I now knew that I was actually going to have to do some marketing. A friend suggested that the best way to market my book would be to get a booth and exhibit at Book Expo America (BEA). What in the world was Book Expo America?

Well, let me tell you that it is an incredible trade show and the largest book publishing event in the United States. 1,500 publishers exhibit, 500 authors participate in book signings, and 20,000 new book titles are featured. Librarians, booksellers, retailers, publishers, agents, and authors all attend. Each year it changes cities, and in 2004 it was being held in Chicago. They charged $3,000 for a booth, and in May I bit the bullet and decided to go for it!

It was also in May that I found this pitcher at a garage sale for $2. It was partial payback for the huge set of the same patterned calico chintz dinnerware that I had missed at that house sale! I know, I know—I said I would drop it. But just this one last time!

While I was putting this pitcher on eBay, I was also getting ready to exhibit at BEA. I had ordered a huge 10' by 15' banner for the back of my booth and printed press releases, business cards and brochures. I had also talked my best friend from high school, Melanie Souve, into flying from Philadelphia to help run the booth for three days.

My dad was in town to take care of my kids so that I could attend. He had ulterior motives, as Houston was finishing up his baseball season and my dad wanted to see that. Houston was also nominated for an all-star summer team, so we were on pins and needles waiting to see if he would be chosen.

Melanie and I had so much fun in Chicago. The booth turned out great and we made so many new friends. Chicago is a wonderful city! Great things happened at BEA. The most important thing I learned was that to get your self-published books into any major store, you now needed a middleman—a distributor. Big stores weren't as willing to buy directly from small independent publishers like me as they had been before. Self-publishers had to be represented by one of the big distributors such as Midpoint or Biblio.

I was able to get a meeting with Midpoint and they agreed to take my book. It was great! I also met Emily Kelly, who works with BAF (Books are Fun), a Reader's Digest company, and she thought my products would be great for a test. All in all, it was a very successful show and this little pitcher ended up selling for $78.10. That was going to pay for about 2.6% of my BEA booth. I had better find some more stuff! And, oh yeah—while I was at BEA, I got the phone call that Houston made the all-star team. Life was good!

#43 St. John Knit Suit

$35.⁰⁰
Paid

From: Consignment store going out of business

St. John Knit Lime Green Spring Suit 3 Pcs As New 12 WOW

Description:
This is a wonderful suit in "as new" condition. It is St. John Collection by Marie Gray. There is a size large short-sleeve jacket with logo buttons. A size medium shell tank and a size 12 skirt. Very nice!

Winning Bid: **$480.⁰⁰**

Ended: 6/7/04
History: 12 bids
Starting Bid: $99.99
Winner: Illinois

Viewed
 **X**

St. John Knit Suit   #43

The Story

One weekend my mom and I ventured over to Palm Springs to check out their garage sales. In late May and the summer months, there are not many garage sales out here in the desert. High season is over and most of the snowbirds have left. It gets trickier and trickier to find good merchandise, so we decided to give Palm Springs a shot.

One of the ads in the paper was for a clothing consignment store that was going out of business. These sales can be very lucrative if the sellers are motivated. Even store clearance sales can be great. I know a lot of bargains went out our shop's front door when we started doing our 40% off sales in 1996. This store still had a lot of merchandise left tagged at the original high store prices. The shop owner told us that if we found anything we were interested in, she would make us a good deal.

I found this lime green St. John Knit three-piece outfit. It was priced at $175. I asked, "How much?" and the owner said, "How about $35?" That is still a lot of money for something I know relatively nothing about. Clothing is not my area of expertise! But I knew St. John was a great brand name and that there was a huge following for their clothing. I also knew that some of the outfits sold in the $1,000 range when new.

St. John, it turns out, is an American classic. The company was founded in 1963 (hey—by the way, so was I) by Robert and Marie Gray. Marie, then a young model, was inspired by a knitting machine to design dresses for herself. Interest from her friends was immediate, and soon after, specialty stores inquired about placing orders. Marie's husband, Robert, saw the strong business potential and today St. John is headquartered in Irvine, CA, and employs 4,000 people. Angelina Jolie was named their spokesmodel in 2006.

It was slim pickings that Saturday in Palm Springs, so I sprang for the St. John Knit at $35. I had to have something to put on eBay that week while I was in Chicago for Book Expo America. I put the suit on eBay with five pictures. I figured that since clothing wasn't my niche and I wasn't very good at describing it, I had better let five pictures tell a thousand words. Or would it be five thousand words?

I couldn't decide whether to start the auction at $49.99 or $99. I wanted to protect my $35 investment and still guarantee a good return. So I chose a $99 starting price. If it didn't sell at $99, I planned to relist it with a cheaper starting bid.

Amazingly enough, that outfit got twelve bids and sold for $480 while I was in Chicago at the Book Expo. Now that was more like it. 16% of my booth price had been covered! I was getting closer and closer to breaking even.

#44 Heywood-Wakefield Chairs

$80.00 Paid

From: Garage sale

Set 4 Signed Heywood-Wakefield Period Chairs Eames MOD!

Description:
Great set of 4 signed Heywood-Wakefield chairs. The two armchairs are 33 ½" by 23" by 20 ½". The two side chairs are 32 ½" by 18" by 19.5". Signed with the Heywood-Wakefield eagle and "Established 1826." I am guessing that these are circa 1940 to 1950. Sleek and very Eames-era, Danish modern (although made in Gardner, Massachusetts). I am guessing that the finish is "wheat" and that the wood is solid birch. The pattern looks like it may be "wink," "slit," or "eye."

Winning Bid:

$204.52

Ended: 6/17/04
History: 6 bids
Starting Bid: $149.00
Winner: California

Viewed

000275 X

The Story

I was deep into writing *How to Sell Antiques and Collectibles on eBay.... and Make a Fortune,* but still putting 100 new things up for sale on eBay each week. How can you write a book about selling on eBay if you aren't really doing it? I was in the middle of the furniture chapter. Of all the antiques categories I was writing about, furniture was my least favorite.

I was stuck. I needed an item I could feature in the furniture chapter. I had an impending deadline to meet, but instead of staying at home writing, I went out to garage sales on Saturday morning with my mom. At one garage sale, I spotted this set of four chairs. They were priced at $80, and when I turned them over I found a signature up inside the frame. It said "Heywood-Wakefield." I asked my mom, "Isn't that a good Eames-era brand?" She said, "Yes, but I don't know if you can get over $80 for them on eBay."

I was in a pickle, but here was a solution (or so it seemed). I thought that even if they didn't sell for much more than $80, it would still be a great example for the book. I bought the chairs and raced home to put them on eBay. I needed the results for the furniture chapter as soon as possible. I listed them at 11:28 AM that Saturday morning. I started the auction at $149. Amazing what you can do when you put your mind to it!

Heywood-Wakefield began in 1826 in Gardner, Massachusetts. Five Heywood brothers began by manufacturing simple chairs in a small barn. In the late 1800's they joined with the Wakefield Rattan Company (hence the name Heywood-Wakefield). In the 1930's, they launched the "Modern" line, and from 1936 to 1966 produced solid birch, steam bent and sleek blonde furniture. The chairs I found were the epitome of the style produced during that period.

That Sunday I was taking the kids to spend the night at the Ritz Carlton (now The Lodge) in Rancho Mirage. It is an awesome hotel (and one you may remember from the Trista and Ryan "Bachelorette" wedding). In the off months—during the hot summer—you can get a room there for $99 a night. I was treating my kids to a night at the hotel because they hadn't seen me much lately; I had been locked in my office writing for weeks. So we went to the Ritz to have some quality time together and to run the air conditioner like crazy!

It was dusk and we were sitting by the pool. The kids weren't in their bathing suits, but just for fun, I told them that they could jump in with their clothes on. What a blast!

The next day we came down the hill and back to reality. The chairs ended up selling for $204.52 and provided just the fodder I needed for the book! They also paid for our night at The Lodge.

#45 Copper Figurine

$0.00
Paid
From: Inheritance

Copper BOY Marble Bear Totem Wrangell Alaska Vintage!

Description:
Copper top marble bear totem figurine. Says "Wrangell, Alaska"
and "Bear Totem." Totem Pole. A copper top and marble or quartz
stone base. 3 ½" by 1 ⅝" by 1 ⅝". Vintage and very neat. Native
American Eskimo.

**Winning
Bid:**

$105.05

Ended: 6/25/04
History: 2 bids
Starting Bid: $9.99
Winner: Alaska

Viewed
 **X**

Copper Figurine   #45

The Story

I was sitting at my computer relisting one evening. Not everything sells the first time it is put up at auction. Definitely not! Some weeks 90% will sell the first time out, and some weeks 10% will sell. It really varies. I try to relist the items that don't sell right away at a new lower starting price because eBay makes it pretty cheap to do so.

So, there I was on a Friday night (how pathetic!) relisting as fast as the auctions were ending, but I had gotten a little ahead of myself. I input an item number and the auction for this totem pole figurine returned, showing that there were ten seconds left and no bids. I waited ten seconds and input the item number again. This time an auction popped up for an item that had sold for over $100. I decided I must have input the wrong number. I tried again and the same auction came up. I couldn't believe it, but when I looked closer I realized it was my listing! This figurine had gone from $9.99 and no bids to $105.05 in the final few seconds.

I still don't know why this piece sold for so much. There were only two people who bid on it, but that is all it takes! I did some research on my own (after the fact) to figure it out. If I had done this before I listed this item, I would have known that the figure was a man, not a boy, and that he was a gold-miner—part of the huge gold rush to hit Wrangell, Alaska. Some of the sources I looked at said that Wrangell was now a ghost town. Interesting!

Here's why I didn't bother doing any research before I listed him. He had been priced at $8.75 in my grandmother's handwriting. This meant that he had been in the shop for at least ten years and did not even sell when priced at 70% off, or $2.62. I didn't think he warranted much time. And to be honest, I can't research everything in depth or I would not be able to list 100 new things each week.

So, I let eBay bidders do research and pricing for me on some things. I wonder what he would have sold for if I had listed him as a gold prospector from an Alaskan ghost town—oooh, spooky! It might have been a lot more... or not. You just never know with eBay. I will tell you that I was thrilled to get over 50 times what he was priced for at clearance in our store!

I just received more information from Trisha Neal, a historian for the town of Wrangell, Alaska. She let me know that Wrangell is a small town of 2,000—not a ghost town yet! She also told me that the bear totem on the shield is probably from the Bear Totem Store in Wrangell that closed in the 1930's. She sent me a picture postcard of the original store. How cool is that?

S-288 The Bear Totem Store - Wrangell, Alaska

Photo used by permission of Schallerer Photo, Ketchikan, AK

#46 Gold Watch Fob

$0.⁰⁰ Paid

From: Inheritance

Antique Victorian Watch Fob GOLD Floral 1880s WONDERFUL

Description:
Antique Victorian Watch Fob Gold Floral 1880's Wonderful. You rarely find these authentic antique watch fobs in gold. It is circa 1880's to 1890's and has been tested for gold. It is! Floral with LJC engraved (I think). It is 1 ⅝" by ⅞" by ½". Priced at $150 in our antiques store. We have a lot of jewelry up for auction this week and it has all been examined or tested by my Gemological Institute of America-certified brother.

Winning Bid:

$67.⁰⁰

Ended: 7/9/04
History: 6 bids
Starting Bid: $24.99
Winner: Texas

Viewed
 X

The Story

I was getting ready to leave for New York for the RTIR (Radio Television Interview Report) Publicity Summit as this auction was ending. The Publicity Summit was going to put 100 authors face-to-face with top media, publicists and agents from around the country. It cost $5,000 to attend and I had decided that 2004 was going to be my year to spend the money and make my book a best seller. My dad was in town for Houston's 8th birthday, so I asked him if he would mind watching the kids. Of course not!

It was so exciting preparing for the Summit. Prep included telephone calls with a former "Dateline" producer, a current "Regis & Kelly" producer and a founder of RTIR. I had advertised with RTIR for years. They put out a bi-monthly magazine that puts you in front of a lot of media. I have gotten a ton of incredible press, radio and television from advertising with them. I was ready for the Summit! Plus, I would be meeting tons of other authors just like me. It was going to be a blast.

This watch fob was in one of the boxes that I inherited from my grandmother. I put it on eBay with a starting price of $49.99 in June. No one bid on it, so I lowered the starting bid price to $24.99 in July. Watch fobs were part of a gentleman's pocket watch ensemble starting back in the late 1800's. The pocket watch would be carried in a fancy vest pocket. To make it easily accessible it was sometimes attached to a leather strap on which hung a piece known as a watch fob. The fob was designed to pull the watch from the pocket. Remember, this was back when people actually dressed up and before wrist watches!

So, my dad is driving me to the airport for my 7 AM flight to NY, and as we turn a corner I hear a strange noise like a helicopter right above our heads. "Dad, what is that?" He says, "I don't hear anything." Keep in mind that he is losing his hearing. Oh my gosh. We figure out that it is a flat tire, and I have a plane to make. Yikes! We call BMW of North America and find that my roadside assistance warranty has just expired. We call AAA. Too long of a wait.

We call my mom who is at my house watching the kids and she throws them in her minivan and comes to get me. We leave my dad there at the side of the road changing the tire. I love my dad. Anyway, I make my flight and have an incredible time in NY. I got to have lunch with producers from "The View" and a dinner meeting with producers from "Oprah". I met incredible authors like Stephen Shapiro (*Goal Free Living*) and Sherri Caldwell (*The Rebel Housewife*) who are still good friends today. It was so worth the money.

Talking about money brings me back to the watch fob. After I relisted it at a lower price, it sold for $67 and went to Houston, Texas. Such a great name for a city—or a kid!

#47   Scuba Fins

$10.⁰⁰
Paid
From: Garage sale

US Diver Snorkeling Diving Set-Fins Mask Snorkel-MIP 8

Description:
US Diver Snorkeling Diving Set-Fins Mask Snorkel-MIP fin size 6.5 to 8. Yellow. Package says "Tempered Aqua Lung Fins Mask Snorkel, Cozumel, Sea Breeze, Dry Allegre." Has never been used but the top was cut off.

Winning Bid:

$68.³⁷/2

Ended: 7/12/04
History: 3 bids
Starting Bid: $9.99
Winner: Missouri

Viewed

000045 X

The Story

I was at a garage sale and saw two sets of snorkeling gear. Ever since I started scuba diving, I immediately hone in on these types of items. Both sets were brand new and mint in the original plastic cases. In fact, they both had the receipts with them. One was from Big 5 and the other was from Sportsmart. Each had cost $49.99 new and had been paid for in cash.

I asked, "How much?" The man wanted $5 for each one. That seemed really fair so I bought them both. I got them home and realized that they hadn't been purchased that long ago—only about four months prior. I had a brilliant idea—why not call the stores and see if I could get a merchandise credit for each one? That would be $100 towards sporting goods for my son. He is an amazing baseball player and I spend a lot of money at Big 5 and Sportsmart.

From my years of being in retail, I knew exactly how to approach this opportunity. As you know, I grew up helping in and eventually running my grandmother's antiques store. I was also an executive trainee for May Department Stores and worked for them for five years. During that time, I was a department manager, an assistant buyer and a buyer. So I knew what to do.

I called both stores first and asked about their return policies. Both allowed cash back up to 30 days after purchase and merchandise credit up to 90 days. Well, my receipts were 120 days, so I asked to speak to the managers. If you are super nice, call ahead, and ask to speak with a manager, you can often get a store to be flexible about its published policies. Remember, you attract more flies with honey than with vinegar. I told both managers that I would be happy with an in-store credit. I did not want a refund. Sportsmart said no to any type of return. To my delight, Big 5 said an in-store credit would be fine.

Luckily, my dad was still in town, so I sent him off to Big 5 with instructions to exchange the snorkeling set for two pairs of white baseball pants for Houston. I couldn't believe it when he walked in the door with no baseball pants but $53.86 in cash! Big 5 did not have any baseball pants because it was off season, so they gave my dad the money! Amazing.

I had made $43.86 on this transaction already and still had another set of snorkeling gear to sell on eBay. The second set did not sell for anywhere near the original retail price, but it added another $14.51 to my overall profit. Grand total profit on this transaction: $58.37. My dad couldn't believe I had the gall to return the items, or that Big 5 actually gave us cash! Luckily, my dad was there to do my dirty work—just as he was always around to spend time with us—even if it was just to fly a kite.

#48 Arabia Coffee, Cream/Sugar

$8.⁷⁵ Paid

From: Thrift store

Early Arabia Finland Chocolate Coffee Pot Side Handle
Arabia Finland Creamer Sugar Art Deco Antique RARE

Description:

This coffee pot is signed with "Arabia" in script on the base. Hand painted art deco design in burnt orange and green. There is a "WX" also painted on the base. There is a crack across the base of the pot and down the side. There is also a chip on the spout. 5 ½" by 5 ½". A very rare piece that I would guess dates to the 1890's to 1900's. This will make a great cabinet piece. We have the matching creamer and sugar also up for sale this week in a separate auction.

Winning Bid: **$597.⁵¹/2**

Ended: 7/15/04
History: 38 bids/2
Starting Bid: $9.99 each
Winners: Finland, Virginia

Viewed

000439 X

Arabia Coffee, Cream/Sugar #48

The Story

Before leaving for New York and the media summit, I had been hitting my local thrift stores. I was going to miss a weekend of garage sale shopping and wanted to make sure I had some good stuff on eBay while I was gone. In the very hot summer months when not many people are around, these stores sometimes have unadvertised sales.

When I walked in to my favorite thrift store, I checked the announcement board and found that the entire store would be 50% off for the month of July. Score! I decided to check out all the items in the locked cases. Typically, these are way overpriced, but at half off, maybe I could make some money. I had been looking at a red and green antique creamer, sugar and coffee pot for almost two years. It was priced at $17.50 for the set and was signed "Arabia." The problem with the set was that all three pieces had chips or cracks or both. At $8.75, I decided to take a chance, and boy am I glad that I did!

The Arabia signature can throw some people off because it sounds Middle Eastern, but it is actually used by a Scandinavian maker. The older pieces of Arabia were just signed "Arabia" and the newer ones are signed "Arabia Finland." In 1873, Rorstrand of Sweden founded a factory in the "Arabia" district of Helsinki, Finland—hence the name Arabia. Arabia is still in business today and is ranked in the top ten of the most valued trademarks in Finland. It is a very good brand and I have had extremely good luck with Arabia pieces.

So I put these on eBay in two separate auctions scheduled to end while I was in New York. Since I had only paid $8.75 total, I started each auc-

tion at $9.99. "A bold strategy, Cotton; I wonder if it pays off for them?" (my daughter's favorite line from "Dodgeball").

Boy, did it pay off for me. Keep in mind that these pieces were not perfect—in fact they were very "as is." The creamer and sugar ended up selling for $290.51 and the chocolate pot for $307. Most of the bidders were from Finland!

I was back from New York and my office phone rang. It was Rachel and Patrick, the producers from "The View." How exciting! They wanted to pitch me to the head of ABC network for a chance to be on "The View" with all those great ladies. What an opportunity.

Rachel and Patrick wanted to know if I had any exciting items that had sold on eBay that I could bring with me as props. Amazingly enough, I did! I emailed the buyers of the Arabia pieces to see if they could wait an extra week to receive their merchandise. Both buyers said, "No problem."

I was all set to go on "The View." Unfortunately, the head of ABC decided not to do the piece. I was bummed! But as my grandmother used to say, "Hang in there—it always works out for the best."

Hang in there, Ol' Buddy!

Lovya lots lil' partner Grandma

#49 Jadite Coffee Mug

$0.**00** Paid

From: Inheritance

OvenWare Fire King Jadite Mug C Handle Heavy Restaurant

Description:
This mug is signed on the base "Oven Ware Fire King". It is 3 ⅜"
by 3 ¼". I think it is a C shaped handle. It is thick and heavy—probably for restaurant use. It is in very good condition with no chips, no
cracks, no crazing. It does have slight wear and is slightly rough.

Winning Bid: **$36.****00**

Ended: 7/30/04
History: 10 bids
Starting Bid: $9.99
Winner: Japan

Viewed
000044 **X**

The Story

I have never had a cup of coffee in my life. OK, I take that back. I had one cup of coffee in Paris in 1985, and it was laced with brandy. It was snowing, I was freezing, and my friends Juliette and Vicki said it would warm me up. It did warm me up, but I still can't stand the taste of coffee. Instead, I drink about six Diet Cokes every day to get my dose of caffeine.

It's funny, but I didn't realize where I learned NOT to drink coffee until I was writing this story. This jadite green coffee mug was in my grandmother's kitchen cupboard for years and years. It finally dawned on me that my grandmother NEVER drank coffee. No wonder I had no desire to try it or like it. I was following the lead of my favorite role model.

Anyway, I inherited it in one of my boxes. I thought one coffee mug was never going to sell for very much, but decided to do some research anyway. I knew it was jadite by Fire King. Fire King was a group of ovenproof lines launched by Anchor Hocking in the early 1940's. Jadite was named for its green color which resembled jade; it became a signature item of the Fire King line. When I got on eBay, I found that these are super collectible. Three of the jadite coffee mugs together had recently sold for $100! Each mug's handle curve is named for different letters of the alphabet—there are "c" and "d" curves. I guessed that mine was a "c" handle.

I put it on eBay with all of that information in the title. I started the bidding at $9.99 (my usual) and couldn't believe it when it got ten bids and sold for $36. It was shipped to Japan and the buyer paid $14 more for airmail shipping. My grandmother would have laughed and laughed over this one. She would have gotten such a kick out of it!

Another thing that she would have gotten a big kick out of was that she and I were appearing in an article in the *Antique Trader* that very same week. I had interviewed Sharon Korbeck, the editor of the *Antique Trader,* for my McGraw Hill book, and she thought that my grandmother and I would make a great story. It was written in the spring of 2004 and published at the end of July.

The *Antique Trader* was my grandmother's favorite magazine; she read it faithfully cover to cover every week. She would have been thrilled to pieces to be featured in this publication. I now include this wonderful article in each box that I ship out to my eBay buyers. I have heard such nice comments from my customers. Things like, "The article adds such a personal touch," and "I feel like I know you and your grandma!" I'll bet they don't know that neither of us ever drank coffee!

#50 Circus Tiger Bank

$0.^{**00**} **Paid**

From: Kiki inherited

Cast Iron Figural Tiger Circus Still Bank Antique RARE

Description:
This is a very rare still antique bank in the shape of a tiger. He still has most of his original paint. He measures 4 ¼" by 4 ½" by 2 ½". Comes from our grandmother's personal collection of antique banks. In very good to excellent condition for his age. I am guessing 1880's to 1900's. Very hard-to-find piece.

Winning Bid: **$1852.**^{**00**}

Ended: 8/15/04
History: 17 bids
Starting Bid: $99.00
Winner: Connecticut

Viewed
 **X**

Circus Tiger Bank #50

The Story

Each summer we try to spend as much time as we can in Bellingham, Washington. The desert gets too hot—120 degrees is typical—and one month my power bill was over $800, mostly from air conditioning. Time to blow out of town. We were up in Bellingham for several weeks during the summer of 2004 and it was great because we got to see the graduations of both Brianne (our former nanny) and Kiki (my sister). Both were getting master's degrees, Brianne in audiology and my sister in social work. What accomplishments!

My sister was throwing a huge party that was going to cost several thousand dollars. She needed to raise money, so I told her that I would help her put some stuff on eBay. We picked out ten really nice things that she had inherited from our grandmother and we listed them on eBay in auctions that were scheduled to end the day before her party. Talk about cutting it close!

Of the ten items, I thought that a Vienna Bronze figurine (like #38) would sell for the most. This tiger bank was cute, but I never thought that it would be worth more than $100. I didn't realize that there was such a following for this type of bank.

We got the ten things on eBay, and off I went for a weekend with my high school girl friends. It was our first get-together since our friend Jodi had died. We were going to go to Nancy Walstrom's cabin on Orcas Island and there were only going to be seven of us. Jodi had been the reason that these girl's weekends had started. I hadn't been a part of the first few, but had been lucky enough to be included for the past several years. They were always so much fun; we would all just sit around and crack up with laughter.

I rode over on the ferry with Karen Bass and Nancy. The weekend was fun, but much quieter and more contemplative than in previous years, when Jodi had been with us. The last time that all eight of us had been together had been a blast, as you can see in the photo.

On Saturday afternoon as we were all sitting around reminiscing about Cadman, my cell phone rang. It was my sister, and she was thrilled to bits to tell me that the circus bank had sold for $1,852. It was going to pay for most of her graduation party.

The gals got a big kick out of hearing this eBay success story. I was sorry to leave them early on Sunday to head back to the mainland by propeller plane for the graduation and party.

My sister and I ended up getting in an argument at her party and we didn't speak for almost a year. Why are families so wonderful and yet so difficult? It seems that the ones we love the most are the ones that we hurt most easily. I am constantly reminded of how short life is when I think of Jodi, so I attempted to patch it up with Kiki many times over that year. One day, she finally called me back, and we are friends again. Time can heal all wounds.

#51 Metlox Cookie Jar

$1.00 Paid

From: Garage sale

Metlox USA Egg Eggs On Basket Cookie Jar Vintage SUPER!

Description:
This great cookie jar is marked "Metlox Made in USA." Eggs on a basket. It measures 9 ½" by 8 ½". In very good to excellent condition. No chips, no cracks. Needs cleaning. Has 3 little felt pieces on the base. Vintage—I would guess 1970's but can't be certain. Would make a great addition to a hen, rooster or chicken collection.

Winning Bid: **$33.99**

Ended: 8/16/04
History: 5 bids
Starting Bid: $9.99
Winner: Iowa

Viewed
 X

Metlox Cookie Jar #51

The Story

I was still in Bellingham for the summer and loving it. When the sun shines, it is not raining, and there is no wind, it is the most beautiful place in the world. Too bad it is only like that for about twenty days each year. (Just kidding—kind of.)

We were enjoying a wonderful summer and there were garage sales aplenty. It is really fun for my mom and I to go out saling in Bellingham because we know all the streets, so we don't have to spend a lot of time mapping out our route or wasting time getting lost! Also, *The Bellingham Herald* (for all its faults) has a great garage sale section that actually divides the sales out by section of town. This is really helpful, and I wish that they would do it in Palm Desert.

Garage saling in Bellingham is also a blast because we run into all sorts of people we know. We typically see antiques dealers, friends from high school, and former customers from the shop. The customers are my favorites, because they all ask how I am doing and we reminisce about my grandmother and the store.

So one Saturday, my mom and I went to a garage sale right across from the beautiful house where my good high school friend Teresa lives with her husband Ken and their two great boys. They also have an amazing house on Eliza Island in the San Juans that I visited recently. Teresa and her family have always been wonderful to me. Teresa's mom, Perk, always used to tell me that I would be very successful and that any time I needed a loan to further a business idea, give her a call. How cool is that to hear when you are twelve?

Anyway, I mentioned to the gal running the sale that Teresa was a good friend. That broke the ice. I was interested in buying this cookie jar, but it was marked "Make Offer." If you know anything at all about me by now, you will know that I HATE those tags! But since we had a friend in common, I thought, "What the heck?" I said, "How much for this jar?" and the gal said, "Hold on—I'll run and ask my mom." She came back and said, "How about $1?" Who ever heard of wasting a "Make Offer" tag on a $1 item? It made absolutely no sense to me, but it worked in my favor that day.

I put it on eBay starting at $9.99. Figural cookie jars, especially those with good brand names, can sell for hundreds of dollars. This one was signed Metlox (which is a super California pottery). I even included the angle that it would work wonderfully with a rooster, hen or chicken collection. There are tons of chicken collectors out there. I was pleasantly surprised when it sold for over $30 and I was able to ship it right from Bellingham to eBay user "cookiejar-jewels" without carting it back to Palm Desert.

#52 Peking Glass Elephants

$0.⁰⁰ Paid
From: Inheritance

Peking Glass White Elephant Mommy Baby Antique Darling!

Description:
This pair of elephants is from 1900's to 1940's. 2 ¼" by 2 ⅛" by ¾" is the Mom elephant. The baby is 1 ¾" by 1 3/4" by ⅝". In great to excellent condition. I could find no chips or cracks. So cute.

Winning Bid:

$36.⁰⁰

Ended: 8/26/04
History: 9 bids
Starting Bid: $9.99
Winner: Oregon

Viewed
 **X**

Peking Glass Elephants #52

The Story

The first summer that we had spent in Bellingham since moving to California was 2003; we were there for eight weeks. I bought everything in Bellingham and then shipped it down in bulk to my assistant Mari, who then shipped out the individual items to each winner. It worked okay, but was a lot of effort and the shipping expenses killed my bottom line.

The summer of 2004, I decided to try something different. I was only going to be in Bellingham for three weeks, so prior to leaving I got 300 items ready to sell on eBay. I wrote up every item on an *i sell* sheet and stored the photos on my laptop. I would list from Bellingham, but all the merchandise would stay in Palm Desert. It was a lot of work up front, but it really paid off. I would still look for great items while in Bellingham.

This darling little set of miniature elephants was in one of the boxes that I inherited from my grandmother. I remember this set being in one of my grandmother's personal cabinets. She loved miniatures, especially animal items. I knew that this would be a popular item because it was both Peking glass and because it involved elephants.

Peking glass is a generic term for subtly colored transparent-to-opaque glass made in mainland China. Glass was probably made in China from as early as 300 BC—although most was made post-1662. Chinese glass was largely designed to imitate more precious metals such as white jade, lapis lazuli and other valuable minerals. I would guess that this Peking glass piece was made to imitate white jade. How neat is that?

There are some interesting myths related to elephant collectibles, as well. The most common is that you should only collect elephants with their trunks up! I should have put that in my title but I didn't know about it at the time I was selling this pair. Experts believe elephants have been used as decoration more than any other animal. Wow!

While in Bellingham, we stayed with my mom at her beach house on Bellingham Bay. It is a beautiful location on 120 feet of low bank waterfront. Unfortunately, there is only dial-up at her house. I had also just received my final review copy of *How to Sell Antiques* and there were pages and pages of author queries to answer. I sat on the beach and did that work, but it would have been an impossible task to list 100 items per week with dial-up—it is too slow. So every morning I would pack up my laptop and head to Kinko's to use their high-speed Internet connection.

It was at Kinko's that I listed this elephant. It ended up selling for $36 while I was still on vacation. Not bad! Over the years, I have found that items will often sell for close to the number of times the auction was viewed. This is why I always put a free visible counter on all of my auctions. I think it encourages people to bid. If they see that a lot of people have already viewed the item, they will realize that they have competition and may bid higher. 42 people looked at this item and it sold for $36—very close to what I would have expected based on my "times viewed" system.

#53 Soft Paste Plate

$0.⁵⁰

Paid

From: Garage sale

Soft Paste Plate 1830's William 4th King Britain RARE!

Description:

This is a really neat little plate. I believe it is soft paste. It has that feel and makes a dull sound when tapped. A picture of William the Fourth, King of Great Britain, is on the front. I believe this was during the 1830's. 6" across. No real chips, no cracks. There is crazing and age discolorations as can be expected. Very neat plate.

Winning Bid:

$143.¹⁰

Ended: 9/13/04
History: 11 bids
Starting Bid: $9.99
Winner: England

Viewed

Soft Paste Plate   #53

The Story

I found this neat little plate at a garage sale in Bellingham. It was marked "50 cents" in what I think of as "old lady handwriting." The plate looked very antique to me, and although I didn't have a lot of experience with soft paste, this plate seemed to match what I had just written for *How To Sell Antiques*. Soft paste is a mixture of clays and glass that produce off-white pieces with small black specks and other imperfections; it was the only way to make a porcelain piece in Europe until about 1710. I thought to myself, maybe this is soft paste? I bought it and shipped it down to California to arrive when I returned home.

We were back in Palm Desert and getting into the swing of things again. The kids had returned to school; Houston had Mrs. Cox for second grade and Indy had Mrs. Gatherum for kindergarten. Awesome teachers! Life was again back to normal except for my super-messy house. I had gone without a housekeeper for about six months in an effort to save money, but I was ready to hire someone.

I asked my assistant Mari if she knew of anyone. She got a funny look on her face and said, "Lynn, I need to talk to you." Oh no! My semi-perfect world was about to become hectic—again. Mari told me that she was taking a job with an accounting firm. She was in school, accounting was her major, and it made a lot of sense for her. I was still very sad. She had been working with me for almost two years. What was I going to do? She said that of course she would help out during the transition, but that they wanted her to start Monday. Monday?! I guessed I would be doing some extra work for a while.

Houston had been invited to play winter baseball (he is an awesome pitcher), and the first day of practice I ran into a bunch of old friends, including Maureen Arcand, Kelly's mom. Houston and Kelly had played on the same team back in 2003 when we had first moved to Palm Desert. I had always liked Mo (short for Maureen) for her biting sense of humor and sarcasm. I mentioned the position to Mo and she seemed interested, but needed time to think about it.

eBay jobs can be great for moms because the hours are totally flexible, and most of the work can be done from home. I kept my fingers crossed and immediately posted a "Help wanted" sign at the local college. Nothing. As the weeks rolled by, I really began to realize what a big job Mari had been doing—and how well she had been doing it.

Anyway, I put this plate on eBay all by myself—even taking the photos! I said that I thought it was soft paste. I couldn't believe it when this 50-cent investment ended up selling for $143.10 and I shipped it back to England. What an incredible find! By the way, I still had a messy house and no assistant—but a 2850% return on my investment made it all bearable.

#54 Backgammon Table

$30.⁰⁰ Paid
From: Thrift store

Eames Era Backgammon Game Table Large Bakelite AMAZING

Description:
This is an amazing folding backgammon game table. It looks to be teak but I can't be sure. Very sleek mod 1950's Eames-era design. The playing surface is cork with black lacquer type edge pieces. The playing pieces are swirl bakelite or catalin in butterscotch yellow and red. They are the extra large size—thick and chunky, great to play with and feel substantial when in your hands. The pieces are about 1 ¾" by ½" thick. Wow! There are 15 of each. This is a pristine complete set. In very good to excellent condition.

Winning Bid:

$295.⁰⁰

Ended: 9/24/04
History: 19 bids
Starting Bid: $49.99
Winner: New York

Viewed

000375 X

Backgammon Table #54

The Story

I was still missing a tire from my car. The spare in my trunk had been used to replace the flat tire I got when I was on my way to catch the plane to New York. I knew it was dangerous to drive without a spare, but I was too busy to deal with this problem! Besides, I was just driving around town.

One of my best friends from college, Juliette Capretta Baia, was having a housewarming party in Newport Beach for an amazing home she had built, and I was invited. Julie and her husband Tony had lived in what amounted to a cracker box for over a year so that they could build their dream home. I wouldn't miss the party for the world. I was really happy for them, but I knew that I had to get a new tire before driving into LA.

I went to a tire store close to my house and just bought one tire. I know, I know—I should have bought four matching tires, but I was short on cash and this is my MO *(modus operandi)*. Just replace what is the most necessary. While I was waiting for the tire to be changed, I wandered over to my favorite thrift store. Amazingly enough, it is in the same strip-mall as the tire place.

I walked in and immediately saw a large backgammon table. It was marked $30 and all the playing pieces were in a Ziploc baggy that I quickly opened so I could feel them. Bakelite or catalin. Score! They were big, thick and chunky—the most desirable type. I also did a count to make sure that they were all there. It's very important for a vintage game to be complete. It was a big piece of furniture, but it folded up and I would be able to ship it by UPS!

I bought it and had them hold it while I went around to pick up my car. I drove over and put it in the trunk. I got home and did my research on eBay. I found that one almost exactly like it had sold on eBay for $155. Mine was in much better condition and I couldn't wait to get it listed. I used six photos and started it at $49.99 with a $35 s/h/i charge.

My mom had agreed to watch my kids and off I went to Newport Beach. Capretta's house was amazing. She had done an awesome job of designing it. The party was packed and it was so fun for me to see her mom Gia, husband Tony, sister Danielle and our good friends Pam and Cliff Cole. I spent the night and got to hang out with them the next day also. It is always wonderful to see Juliette.

The amazing backgammon table sold for $295 the next weekend—almost double the price of the other one. Condition is very important, and I made almost ten times my investment. It is always great when you can do that!

#55 Coral Reef Dinnerware

$10.00 Paid

From: Thrift store

Vernon Kilns Coral Reef Aloha Maroon Cup Saucer Mint

Description:

This beautiful cup and saucer set measures 6 ½" by 2 ⅜". In very good condition. No chips, no cracks, and no crazing. The cup is vivid with some slight fading on the saucer. We have a lot of this china up for auction this week. It is the Coral Reef Aloha pattern by Vernon Kilns and designed by Don Blanding. It is such a neat pattern with fish and sea life. This is a maroon transfer design.

Winning Bid: **$284.06/12**

Ended: 10/27/04
History: 44 bids/12
Starting Bid: $9.99 each
Winner: CA, NJ, HI

Viewed
000256 X

Coral Reef Dinnerware #55

The Story

I bought a box of china at my thrift store for $10. I loved the pattern—it was very tropical and kitschy. The pieces, however, were pretty ratty. It was seven bread plates and seven cups and saucers. These are not pieces that typically sell for much, and there were a lot of chips. I got it home and started my sorting process. I typically throw away (or donate to charity) any really damaged pieces. I started weeding through the box and had a pile of six pieces that I put in my garbage can.

Then I sat down at my computer and pulled up the Replacements web site. This was a rare pattern! Replacements had none listed in stock for sale. I got on eBay and found that a chipped dinner plate had recently sold for $39. I couldn't get to my garbage can fast enough to pull out those chipped pieces!

Don Blanding designed these for Vernon Kilns. Vernon Kilns began as Poxon Pottery in 1916 in Vernon, California. The name was changed to Vernon Kilns when it was sold to Faye Bennison in 1931. She began hiring celebrated artists for the company's new designs. Among those artists were Walt Disney and Don Blanding. Don Blanding was quite a character. He was known as the "Vagabond Poet" and lived from 1894 to 1957. He was the author of such classics as *Hula Moons* and *Drifter's Gold*. Blanding began designing for Vernon Kilns in 1938 from his redwood bungalow in Carmel, California. It was in his studio in that 'Vagabond House' that he designed Coral Reef. It became ex-

tremely popular and collectible and was so unique in the marketplace that it had no equal during the 1930's to 1950's. Vernon Kilns went out of business in 1958. Amazing—no wonder it was such a hot pattern!

I have to tell you that after I had made it through six weeks with no assistant, my friend Maureen (Mo) finally decided to give it a shot. I was so excited! We had worked out all the details, one of which was that she would keep her waitressing job. Mo had been waiting tables for twenty years and was really ready to give a different career a try, but we agreed that she should keep her lunch shift in case this didn't work out for us.

eBay involves a lot of detail-oriented tasks, so the first month was really all learning. Maureen was doing a great job and seemed to enjoy the work. I had a good feeling about her (and still do!). She is also quite the character and we laugh a lot. Her son's school was right across the street from my house, which made the job even better for her. She was also able to do a lot of the work from home at night.

Anyway, while I was teaching Maureen the ropes, this ratty set of china sold for over $280 in twelve separate auctions. A cup and saucer sold for the most at $33.99. Maureen could not believe that these chipped and faded pieces sold for so much! Quite frankly, neither could I. FYI, now I don't throw out any defective china until I see how the perfect pieces sell first.

#56 Dansk Pawn Grinders

$4.00 Paid
From: Charity sale

Dansk Salt Pepper Mill Teak Grinder Eames Chess Piece

Description:

Teak salt and pepper mill combination is signed "Dansk Designs Ltd. Thailand." The cork-type top comes off. This is one of the most attractive and collectible shapes and I think it was designed by Jens Quistgaard for Dansk. I believe that it is from the Chess piece collection. Slight wear but no cracks, no splits. The grinding mechanism works perfectly. 7" by 3 ½". We have another similar one also up for sale this week. The wood grain is beautiful on this piece.

Winning Bid: $124.⁹⁹/2

Ended: 11/6/04
History: 26 bids/2
Starting Bid: $9.99 each
Winner: Michigan, Japan

Viewed
000291 X

Dansk Pawn Grinders #56

The Story

It was that season again—Halloween. Time for my favorite charity rummage sale, and once again my mom and I were first in line—along with most of the antiques dealers in the desert. There wasn't as much great stuff this year, but I still found some treasures.

On first glance, I thought that even though these two grinders were both Dansk, they didn't match. They looked like a mismatched salt and pepper shaker. I didn't think that they would sell for much, and they were marked $2 each. Kind of steep. I put them in my box just in case. I could always edit later. I ended up buying them and when I showed them to my mom she was jealous—always a good sign.

It turned out that they weren't a mismatched pair, but in fact two separate self-contained grinders. They each had a top portion for salt and a lower section for grinding fresh pepper. What was really neat was that they were, according to my mom, from the chess piece series done by Dansk. There are a lot of collectors for Dansk chess pieces. Who knew? But I was about to find out.

In the early 1950's, New York entrepreneur Ted Nierenberg and his wife Martha were in Denmark at a Copenhagen museum and spotted a hand-forged metal fork, knife and spoon with teakwood handles. It had been designed by Jens Quistgaard. Quistgaard, born in 1919, is best known for his three-dimensional designs and traditional craftsmanship. His parents were a sculptor and a painter and the famous Georg Jensen, silversmith, was his mentor and teacher. Ted decided that he wanted to mass-produce Jens' flatware pieces.

Quistgaard thought that his pieces would be too difficult to manufacture. Ted convinced him otherwise, and eventually Jens moved to America to help found an American company working in the Danish modern style. That company was Dansk designs, and that first pattern that combined two natural materials in a graceful design was "Fjord." Tabletop had been redefined. What is amazing is that until I wrote this story I had always assumed that Dansk was a Danish company. Never in a million years did I think that it could be American.

The "chess piece" series was mainly designed by Jens Quistgaard, whose JHQ or IHQ mark is often found on the Dansk items he has designed. I put both grinders on eBay to end on the same day and noted in each auction that there was a similar grinder in a separate auction. One ended up selling for $68 and the other for $56.88. I got a really neat email from the guy who bought the $68 grinder, Doug Phillips. It turns out that he is a serious collector and he sent me photos of his collection.

Doug said, "I love the teak mills produced in Denmark. I've been collecting for years and have never found any catalogs showing what was produced, so my collection is the best reference I have. I've tried to help other collectors by sending them pictures of what I know. I have grinders by Nissen, Sottsass, Dansk and unknown." He should write a book!

#57 Baccarat Chandelier

$20.⁰⁰

Paid

From: Charity rummage sale

Antique Baccarat Crystal Prism Chain Chandelier French!

Description:

Antique chandelier is amazing! 7-bulb 1920's large draped lamp fixture. This wonderful piece is signed in the center on a silver metal piece. It has crystal glass detail at the top and base. The all-over prisms and chains are mostly original! Very few of the original crystals have been replaced. It is entirely complete with 60 chains of crystals prisms around the base and another 60 at the top. It needs a cleaning. 34" from base to top.

Winning Bid: **$2,284.⁰⁰**

Ended: 11/12/04
History: 24 bids
Starting Bid: $249, $1995 rsv
Winner: Japan

Viewed

000452 X

Baccarat Chandelier #57

The Story

At that same charity sale, I spotted a lamp under a table. It was mainly prisms and marked $20. I dragged it over to my pile behind the cashiers. It looked slightly bent, but any lamp with prisms is worth a shot. Remember, I sell new prisms for 99 cents each, and this one had hundreds on it. The lamp was quite large and heavy.

Once I had it in my pile, an antiques dealer came up to me and said, "I will give you $100 for that lamp." "No way," I said. He said, "How about $200?" "No, I really want it." Whenever anyone tries to buy something from you at a charity or garage sale, you know that you have something great! How exciting.

That lamp sat in my dining room for two weeks before I attempted to check it out; I knew getting it ready to sell would be a full day's project. When Maureen and I finally took it outside and started hooking on the prisms, I looked at the base and happened to spot a metal button with a signature. I said, "Oh, my gosh." Maureen said, "What—what is it?" I couldn't believe the name. Baccarat.

Maureen asked, "What is Baccarat?" Just one of the most important French crystal companies ever! Baccarat was founded as a glass works in 1764 in the village of Baccarat. In 1816 it produced its first crystal. Over the years, Baccarat has become famous for wonderful perfume bottles and stemware. What a score!

As soon as I saw the Baccarat signature, I raced to my computer to start my research. I couldn't find anything on eBay for "Baccarat chandelier," which meant that they were pretty rare. I got on Google to do my research and found one that had sold in 1995 for $3,680. It was quite similar, but was about ten inches bigger than mine and had twelve lights rather than seven. I estimated that $2,000 would be a fair price. I got so caught up in the research that I forgot I had left Maureen outside holding the lamp. Oops!

I started the bidding at $249 with a reserve of $1,995. It reached its reserve after just three days. How awesome. With four minutes left, it was still at $1,995. I kept refreshing my auction page; there was no change until it went to $2,284 with four seconds remaining. Wow!

We quoted the buyer $240 for air-mail shipping to Japan. Can you believe that? I bubble-wrapped each and every prism—it took me about four hours. We shipped it in two boxes that cost $211.30 at the post office. While I was packing it, my favorite cross got caught on the metal frame, and when I stood up the chain and the bale broke. The cross was a rose cut diamond piece of art from the 1840's that my grandmother had bought in Russia. Another job hazard.

I was really nervous waiting to see if the lamp arrived safely. I received an email from the buyer saying everything was great but there was a slight chip in the glass font. I knew that filing a claim with the post office would be fruitless, so I asked him what would make him happy. He wanted a partial refund of $200. I quickly agreed and realized that it had sold for $2,084 after my refund. Even after paying $45 to have my cross and chain repaired, I still netted $2K. What an awesome item! I wish these would come along a lot more often.

#58 Abelman Paperweight

$15.⁰⁰

Paid

From: Garage sale

Stuart Abelman Art Glass Vintage Paperweight 1980 RARE

Description:

Wonderful paperweight is Forget Me Not Floral iridescent Old studio weight. This piece is signed "Abelman 1980 IG4-176." It is a beautiful piece. The flower is pink, purple, greenish blue and turquoise. There is also cobalt blue at the edges. It is amazing. This is a rare early piece that was done just 3 years after Stuart opened Abelman Art Glass. This piece is in excellent condition and measures 3" by 2" ¾". This piece looks just like an Orient & Flume design.

Winning Bid:

$110.⁵¹

Ended: 11/14/04
History: 19 bids
Starting Bid: $9.99
Winner: Pennsylvania

Viewed

000199 X

Abelman Paperweight #58

The Story

I was out garage saling (or is it sailing?) all by myself. Boo hoo. I found this paperweight priced at $15 and it was beautiful. I asked the lady if she would take $10. "No way," she said. I had seen an etched signature on the base, but didn't recognize the name. It was done in the style of Orient and Flume, which I knew very well because my grandmother collected it. Orient and Flume was founded in 1972 in Chico, California; they reproduced natural designs in both iridescent and crystal clear glass. But not recognizing this signature, I passed and walked out to my car.

As I started my car, I could hear my grandmother saying to me, "If you love something, you should buy it." She was right—the piece was stunning, and $15 was not too much to pay if I decided to keep it. Actually, if I was buying for myself, $15 was cheap. I got out of my car and paid the $15.

I got on eBay as soon as I got home to research the signature, "Abelman." I found that Stuart Abelman had attended Carnegie Mellon University and received a Bachelor of Fine Arts. He went on to earn a Master of Fine Arts in Glass at UCLA. He was a pioneer in the art glass movement of the 1960's, His studio was founded in 1977—so this piece was made only three years after opening.

Stuart is highly respected in the art glass world and his pieces are prized by collectors. Works created at Abelman Art Glass are in demand, not only for the technical expertise required to produce them, but for their creativity and originality. Abelman's works are displayed in galleries, museums, and private collections around the world. He has done commissions for Sunset Magazine, the White House, gourmet restaurants, the House of Blues and the Disney Company. Wow!

I found that Abelman's paperweights usually bring in more than $100, so I decided to sell this one. Paperweights are very collectible; they are rarely used to hold down papers, but are appreciated instead for their fine workmanship and beauty.

Paperweight collectors recognize three periods of paperweight production. The "classic period" began in 1840 and ran through 1880. Famous paperweight companies are St. Louis and Baccarat (both French), and U.S. companies Boston & Sandwich and Pairpoint. The second "folk art and advertising" period ran from the 1880's to the 1940's; it saw the decline of major factories and the growth of small, family-run factories. The final "contemporary period" began after World War II, and features the "studio glass" artist, who works alone in a studio using the early techniques of the classic period.

My paperweight was definitely from the contemporary period and was certainly a studio piece. I started the auction at $9.99 to encourage bidding. It received nineteen bids and this Abelman piece ended up selling for $110.51. Thank goodness I listened to the little voice in my head that day.

You like it, buy it!

#59 18K Coral Ring

$0.⁰⁰ Paid

From: Inheritance

18K Gold Size 8 Coral Cameo Ring Art Nouveau $195 NICE

Description:

18K gold ring was priced at $195.00 in our antiques store. Round carved coral ring. The woman has wavy hair and is very Art Nouveau in look and feel. The size is an 8 to 8 ¼. The top portion is ⅝" round and the ring is ⅜" tall. The cameo looks vintage/antique to me. In great condition. We have a lot of jewelry up for auction. It has all been checked by my brother who is GIA (Gemological Institute of America) certified and we guarantee it all to be as represented.

Winning Bid:

$76.⁰⁰

Ended: 11/24/04
History: 6 bids
Starting Bid: $49.99
Winner: Oregon

Viewed

 X

18K Coral Ring #59

The Story

My brother, Lee, got an undergraduate degree from Western Washington University (WWU) in music. How can you make a living with a music degree? Not easily, as he found out. My grandmother had been trying to get one of her grandkids to go to gemological school forever and ever. Here was her chance.

She told Lee that she would pay for him to go, and my dad also kicked in some cash. Every family needs a doctor, attorney, jeweler, and computer expert, and it looked like we were about to get the jeweler. My brother went off to live in Santa Monica for two years to attend the Gemological Institute of America.

Anyway, my grandmother finally got her jeweler, and I have to admit it has really come in handy over the years. Lee had identified this piece as 18-karat gold, and the carved insert as coral. I thought the style was very Art Nouveau and that the piece was vintage, if not antique. "Art Nouveau" was a style popular between about 1890 and 1914; it is characterized by curving lines and influenced by nature, especially flowers.

When I was writing the first *100 Best* book, my editor, Susan Thornberg, couldn't believe that I was spelling "noveau" like this. She and I have been friends since sixth grade and we lived across the street from one another. Susan emailed me one day and said "If you actually spelled 'nouveau' correctly, you might sell your items for even more." Ha ha, very funny. I got it. Now I spell "nouveau" right every time.

Cameos are a type of carving in which the stone around a design is cut away, leaving the design in relief. Cameos were most often carved from shell and coral, although agate and onyx were also used. Cameos were most popular from about 1870 to the 1930's. This fit in with my "Art Nouveau" style identification.

This ring had been priced in our store at $195, which means that by the time everything was 70% off, it could have been purchased for $58.50. That is why I priced the auction at $49.99 to start. I wouldn't let it go for less than that. I also noted in the title and description that it had been priced at $195 in our store.

The jury is out on whether you should ever list a suggested retail price in an auction. Some people claim that it keeps your item from going over the listed retail price; at the same time, it can actually encourage bidding by making people think they're getting a deal. In this case, since jewelry is a hard sell on eBay, I thought including the retail price would probably help.

However, with my brother's identification, Susan's correct spelling, and a good auction title, this piece sold for $76. I was very happy with that.

#60 Bar Signs

$1.50 Paid
From: Garage sale

Becks Beer Bar Mirror Sign Golf Palm Desert NEAT

Description:
This neat sign says "How About Another Round" Palm Desert. It is a bar mirror by Advanced Mirror Design. In very good to excellent condition. Needs cleaning. 20 ½" by 24 ½". We have a few bar collectibles up for auction this week. Great for a dorm room or bar or pool room.

Winning Bid:

$75.00/2
Ended: 11/27/04
History: 17 bids/2
Starting Bid: $9.99 each
Winner: Maryland, California

Viewed
 X

The Story

Golf is huge here in Palm Desert, as it is in many other places in the world. I turned out for the golf team in high school to meet cute boys. I didn't make the Sehome High School golf team in Bellingham, nor did I meet any cute boys in the process. Oh, well—it wasn't really my sport.

It appears that it is my kids' sport. Here in the Coachella Valley, the Desert Junior Golf Association offers free lessons for kids every Saturday morning. These lessons are such an incredible opportunity that Houston and Indy go most Saturdays. They both have a natural talent and ability, so it is fun to watch. One morning, Houston was hitting the ball so far that the teacher went to get the pro to watch him. The pro said, "I know Houston. He is on my son's baseball team and boy, is he a good athlete." So, my kids are not taking after me and my golf disability. What a relief! Golf really is a good social sport and can help you in both life and business.

The Golf Channel puts on a "Drive, chip and putt" contest that travels around the country. It's free to enter, and it was here in the Palm Desert area in the fall. Indy was too little to participate, but Houston was the right age. He ended up winning a medal in the chipping contest. The Golf Channel had a big celebration and provided free dinner after the day on the course. Palm Desert is an incredible place to live because there are so many wonderful opportunities for children.

It was just after the Golf Channel event that I was out one Saturday morning and found these two signs. I knew that golf and beer collectibles tend to sell well on eBay. In fact, any sports or beer item that can be collected or used to decorate will sell well. There are collectors who look for the advertising items of particular brands. These two signs were at a local garage sale; one was marked 50 cents and the other was $1. I have had good luck with bar signs, so I bought them both. They would have been used originally for advertising within a bar.

The mirrored "Palm Desert Golf" sign ended up selling for the most money—probably because it appealed to collectors of both golf items and beer memorabilia. It had only cost 50 cents, and I couldn't believe it when it sold for $41! The tin "Mexico Bud" beer sign also did quite well, getting up to $34 before the auction ended. Do not overlook any sports memorabilia or bar advertising items when out garage saling. And, if you are good at and enjoy a certain sport, consider specializing in that field on eBay.

#61 Teak Wall Lamp

$3.⁰⁰ Paid
From: Garage sale

1960's Eames Era Danish Swedish Modern Teak Wall Lamp

Description:
This is the neatest wall lamp. It extends to 32". It is teak wood with what looks like a string shade (has a stain/burn mark.) Probably made in Denmark or Sweden. It says "OA 6" on the wood and the lamp shade still has the original manufacturer's tag which is a funky "S." If anyone knows the company we would appreciate knowing. It is 8 ¼" tall. It needs a plug end, so we couldn't test it. It just ends with loose wires. Should be easy to fix.

Winning Bid:

$52.⁰⁰

Ended: 11/29/04
History: 16 bids
Starting Bid: $9.99
Winner: New York

Viewed
 000194 X

Teak Wall Lamp #61

The Story

I am always on the lookout for mid-century modern Eames-era items. This is the period lasting from 1947 to 1969, named for Charles and Ray Eames. These items are super-sleek, retro, and many were made from teak. I particularly like Scandinavian items, because they sell like hotcakes on eBay.

There was an estate sale in Rancho Mirage that advertised very high end, quality items at cheap prices. I was there before it opened, and one of the sellers was outside waiting. She said hello, and I noticed that she had a European accent. I asked her where she was from and she told me she was Swedish. This sale was looking better and better.

When she and her friend finally swung open the garage doors, there were wonderful items inside. There was an Arabia Finland dinner set in blue and white, a lot of teak mid-century items and this lamp. I quickly made a pile and started asking for prices. Nothing was priced too high and the ladies were darling. I bought this lamp for $3.

It was a very unusual piece—a wall fixture that had a fold-out arm that would reach 32 inches when extended. I did some research and found that a very similar one had sold on eBay for $78.77. My lamp had a burn mark on the shade, so I made sure to note this in the description.

I grew up in a house full of teak mid-century modern furniture. My mom and dad had traveled to Denmark in 1960 and brought back living and dining room furniture. The chairs and couches were all sleek, with angular green and amber cushions. These worked quite well with my mother's orange shag carpet. The dining room chairs were teak with black leather backs that would swing back and forth. Lee and I used to line them up and crawl through them, making the chair backs swing, and we would pretend that it was an amusement park ride. We would laugh and giggle until my mom caught us. Do moms always ruin the fun? I'm wondering if I have become a mom who ruins the fun. I hope not.

There was also a huge stereo in Danish teak. I would play the Carpenters on the turntable and sing at the top of my lungs when I had to vacuum. Another one of my chores was raking the shag carpet. Can you believe that people actually raked their carpets? Can you believe that I remember this?

The point of this story is that this type of furniture may be a familiar memory for many of us. And this is what is selling on eBay now. The baby boomers have a lot of money to spend and they are often trying to purchase their childhoods.

This lamp probably reminded someone of days gone by, and even with the burned shade it sold for $52 to a buyer in New York. I just hope that pea green and orange shag carpets don't come back into favor. Yikes!

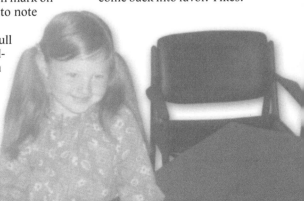

#62 Norwegian Wood Beer Stein

$3.⁰⁰ **Paid**

From: Garage sale

Norwegian Wooden Beer Stein Mug Antique Neat Norway

Description:
This beer stein may be older than Eames Era. I am guessing 1900's to 1940's. It is so cute. The lady we bought it from said it was Norwegian. 6 ½" by 6 ¼" by 4 ½". There is a split in the wood at the handle—nothing major. Wood burned design, black ribbing and it may have had a glass inset. Really super! We bought a lot of really great Eames era (1947 to 1969) items (this one included) from an older Swedish woman. Most are European and very neat.

Winning Bid: **$40.**⁰⁰

Ended: 11/29/04
History: 13 bids
Starting Bid: $9.99
Winner: Wisconsin

Viewed

000136 X

Norwegian Wood Beer Stein #62

The Story

I got this neat stein at the same Swedish lady's sale. She told me that it was Norwegian and she wanted $3 for it. It was unusual because it was made from wood and had some black ribbing around it. I thought it was older than Eames era and eventually dated it from the 1900's to the 1940's.

I do this quite a lot in my listings. I give a date range. If I had said the stein was from 1900 and it was really 1940's, a disappointed buyer might return it. By giving a date range, I am being honest and protecting myself. I will also do this with condition and say something like "in good to very good condition." People's opinions of condition can vary a lot. Just what is "good" and what is "very good"? By giving a range, I let others interpret the true condition (from both the photos and the condition details) so that they feel comfortable bidding.

This piece got quite a bit of play, with 136 people looking at the listing. That is a lot of viewers. It had 13 bids and sold for $40. The best part of this auction was where that beer stein ended up. The buyer was Deb Carey, who, along with her husband, Daniel, own The New Glarus Brewing Company.

Deb and Daniel epitomize American entrepreneurs. Deb raised the capital for the brewery start-up as a gift to her husband, establishing her as the first woman to found and operate a brewery in the U.S. They opened in June of 1993. The brewery has won many awards, including the title of "Best Small Brewery in America" at the Great American Beer Festival in 2003.

Their brewery is located in the outskirts of New Glarus, Wisconsin (hence the name "New Glarus Brewery"). New Glarus has a strong Swiss heritage that is noticeable the minute you set foot into town. There are many antiques stores, two museums, an authentic Swiss bakery and many restaurants that serve genuine Swiss cuisine. As I write this, I am wondering if this stein is more Swiss than Norwegian. It sure could be! The Swedish ladies could have been wrong. Don't believe everything that people tell you—especially when they are trying to sell you something!

Whatever the stein's lineage, I would bet that it has its roots in Europe, just like my family. My grandpa Leaf was 100% Swedish; my grandma was 50% Swedish, 25% Scotch-Irish and 25% English. That made my mom 75% Swedish, 12.5% Scotch-Irish and 12.5% English—and a good-looking family they were! My dad is 50% Norwegian and 50% German. That makes me quite a mixture, but this stein could probably trace its roots back to any of the countries of my ancestors.

Deb told me that this piece now sits in their brewery lunchroom. How cool is that?

#63   1925 RC Christmas Plate

$0.00

From: Inheritance

Royal Copenhagen 1925 Christmas Plate Street Scene Neat

Description:
RC 1925 Christmas plate shows a street scene from Christianshavn, Copenhagen. Designed by Oluf Jensen. The boy is dragging home a Christmas tree. In Denmark, every home must have its tree. Even though a family may be quite poor, there is always at least a small tree. Thousands of trees are imported each year from Norway and Sweden to sell in Copenhagen. This plate is 7" and is in excellent condition. Danish and hand painted in blue and white.

Winning Bid:

$100.00

Ended: 11/29/04
History: 16 bids
Starting Bid: $9.99
Winner: Virginia

Viewed
 X

1925 RC Christmas Plate #63

The Story

I love Danish Christmas plates. My grandmother loved Danish plates also and they were a cornerstone of her business. She began importing them from Denmark in 1960. The tank in the basement was full of collector's plates. It was a fireproof room made of concrete and there were literally stacks and stacks of plates—tens of thousands. So, of course we all inherited quite a few plates and the two main (and best) Danish companies are Royal Copenhagen and Bing & Grondahl.

The tradition of collecting a Christmas plate each year is based on a legend. The wealthy Europeans had a Christmas tradition of giving each of their servants a platter piled high with cookies, candy and fruit. The food was what the gift was all about, so they didn't really take notice of the plate. It is believed that the first platters were made of wood. Since the servants did not have much, they began hanging these platters on their walls for decoration and they began referring to them as Christmas plates.

The servants began to compete amongst one another to see who had the best plate each year. The rich Europeans began to spend more and more money on the plate and less on the food that came on it. At some point, they began dating the plates so that they could remember which one came during which year. This is where the custom began.

Bing & Grondahl (B & G) was the first Danish company to begin mass-producing Christmas plates in 1895. Harald Bing, then the head of the company, came up with this idea. He had no concept of the huge trend he created with the selling of these annual collectibles. The first plate said "Jule Aften 1895," meaning "Christmas Eve 1895." The scene was called "Behind the Frozen Window" and it is a beautiful plate. I only sold two of these plates while running my grandmother's antiques store, and they brought in over $5,000 each.

Royal Copenhagen (RC), then a rival of B & G, began issuing the same type of Christmas plate in 1908. Their first plate was called "Madonna and Child." When we sold these in the antiques store, they were priced at about $3,000.

Both companies continue to produce these plates each year. The blue and white plates are still hand-painted and every year after Christmas, the molds are destroyed to enhance the value by preventing any future reproductions. About four years ago, the two companies merged, but they still issue plates under their original names.

My grandmother always tried to have at least one plate from each year hanging on the wall in the shop. This was about 100 plates for each line. They looked so great hanging on the white walls. I loved looking at them while growing up, and reading the story behind each year's motif. This plate came in one of the boxes that I inherited. It had been priced at $119 and had hung on the wall of the shop for four years. I was very pleased when it sold for $100!

#64 Groovy Boy Sean

$5.⁰⁰ Paid

From: Shop purchased

Groovy Girls Manhattan Toy Sean Retired Boy Doll MWT

Description:
Groovy Girl doll, Sean, the boy, is blond and has "fuego" written on his shirt. These dolls are all brand new and mint with tags. 13". We have a lot of Manhattan Toy Company Groovy Girl Dolls and clothes up for sale this week. They are all in perfect condition and I believe that they are all retired. These were brought brand new in the late 1990's for our antiques and gift store and have been boxed.

Winning Bid:

$20.⁵⁰

Ended: 12/9/04
History: 8 bids
Starting Bid: $9.99
Winner: Michigan

Viewed
 000037 X

Groovy Boy Sean   #64

The Story

This story is also about something that we used to carry in the shop—Groovy Girl dolls and accessories. Manhattan Toy Company came out with this really fun line in the late 1990's. We were looking for something to replace the Ty Beanie Babies that were so rudely taken away from us, and we came across this incredible line. We had a room in the shop solely devoted to this fun merchandise.

The room that housed the "Groovies" was called the "middle bedroom" and actually used to be my mom's room when she was in high school. She dated my dad when this was her bedroom. How strange! Later in its history, it became my grandmother's bedroom. After the addition was built on, it became a stockroom. When I moved home to run the store in 1993, I decided that we would expand the shop, and the logical place to start was to go down the old hall and into the old bedrooms—"middle bedroom" included.

It was a big project, but when the old pink walls were finally painted white and new carpet had been laid, the room was great for selling toys! We always secretly (okay, not secretly—quite verbally) hoped that these would become as popular and as collectible as Beanie Babies.

Manhattan Toy Company was founded in 1979 by Francis Goldwyn, grandson of motion picture studio owner Sam Goldwyn. Goldwyn is no longer involved with the ownership of Manhattan Toy, but the company claims that they "remain true to his vision of marching to the beat of a different (toy) drum." I like that vision, and my grandmother did also.

Funny thing, as I am writing this and see the name Sam Goldwyn, I am reminded of a piece that my grandmother gave me. It is a guilloche French compact that once belonged to Mrs. Samuel Goldwyn (Frances Howard Goldwyn), the great grandmother of the man who founded Manhattan Toy Company. My grandmother gave me this wonderful piece that she bought in the 1970's for $25, and it comes with an affidavit from Mrs. Goldwyn's personal secretary saying that it belonged to the movie mogul's wife.

I will never really know if it belonged to Mrs. Goldwyn, but it is a lovely compact and lipstick that hang from a finger ring, and I treasure this piece of early Hollywood memorabilia. It is something very special.

The Groovy Girls sold great for us when we had the shop, but there were still quite a few left over in our inheritance boxes. For every six to twelve new girl dolls that would be introduced, there would only be one boy. I put this Groovy Girl boy doll named "Sean" on eBay and started him at $9.99. I was thrilled when he sold for $20.50. Maybe, just maybe, these retired Groovies will be worth as much as those Ty Beanies. Now, that would be something!

#65 Westinghouse Insulator

$0.⁰⁰ Paid

From: Inheritance

Blk Ceramic Antique Westinghouse Insulator 1905 Unusual

Description:
This insulator is a very unusual shape. It was originally painted black and most of the paint is missing or worn. Marked "Westinghouse Pat. July 11 1905, S-29865-C" No chips that I can see. 5 ¼" by 3 ½" by 5 ¾".

Winning Bid: **$72.⁹⁹**

Ended: 12/10/04
History: 7 bids
Starting Bid: $9.99
Winner: California

Viewed

X

Westinghouse Insulator #65

The Story

This item was in a box that I got from the shop. It had been priced at $8.50 (in my grandma's handwriting) for years and years! I knew that it was an insulator, and an oversized one at that. I didn't know much about insulators other than they were used in the overhead power lines to regulate the flow of electricity, and that a lot of people collected them.

Over the years helping my G (grandma), I had handled many of the more common turquoise insulators. I knew that they weren't worth a whole lot. But this one was different—it had a very unusual shape, and no damage that I could see. I just had a feeling that it might sell on eBay.

I thought I should find out more about this piece. I started doing research on Google. All of a sudden I found myself back in the lighting/electrical world that I disliked. I ended up in that world after I quit my job as a buyer for the May Company to get my MBA. I had really enjoyed being a buyer and was earning a nice salary, but I thought that an MBA would open some doors for me. When I graduated top of my class—actually, I was honored with the "Outstanding Student Award" at USC for my entire Master's program—I was sure that the MBA would help me land my dream job.

It turns out that my dream job (working for a major movie studio in marketing) would have paid about 50% of my previous salary, and I just wasn't willing to work for that. So I took a position as a buyer (again) at Lamps Plus in Chatsworth. The salary was higher than it had been pre-MBA, so I was happy. But (and this is a big "but") I was buying track and recessed lighting and controls. How boring and outside my comfort zone was that? VERY! To help me get the expertise I needed, Lamps Plus sent me to lighting school every Tuesday night for eight weeks. Even after "graduating," I still just didn't GET IT.

I was pretty miserable buying products I didn't understand, so when my grandmother broke her hip in January of 1993, it pushed me into making a decision. I realized my grandmother was getting older and I wanted to take advantage of the time I had left with her. My grandma and I discussed it at length and she thought she could pay me $10 an hour to help her run the business. At the time, I was making close to $30 an hour. Whatever! I decided to go for it. I put my house on the market and it sold in 22 days. I was Bellingham bound!

Despite my aversion to electrical products I didn't understand, I put this insulator on eBay. It turns out that it was a Porcelain Transformer Cutout that was missing the pull-out switch handle. That didn't seem to matter to the collector who purchased it for $72.99, however. This auction reminded me how happy I am not to be in the lighting business, and how grateful I am that I left LA and spent seven quality years with my favorite person in the whole world—my G!

#66 Vietri Soup Tureen

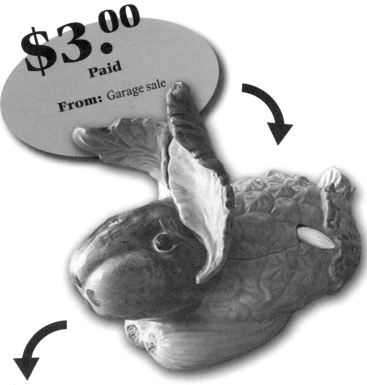

$3.00 Paid
From: Garage sale

Vietri Italian Bunny Rabbit Vegetable Soup Tureen SUPER

Description:
Vietri Italian Bunny Rabbit Soup Tureen is so darling. It is a 3 piece tureen—base, lid, and spoon. The bunny rabbit is made of vegetables—lettuce, cabbage, onions etc. He looks like part of the garden. Needs a cleaning but no chips, no cracks, no crazing. In great shape. Majolica style. Signed "Vietri Made in Italy." 10 ½" by 8" by 5 ¼". Very expensive originally.

Winning Bid:

$79.00

Ended: 12/14/04
History: 23 bids
Starting Bid: $9.99
Winner: Florida

Viewed
 X

Vietri Soup Tureen #66

The Story

I was at a garage sale with my mom and saw this rabbit on the ground. It was priced at $3. I turned it over and saw that the signature was "Vietri, Italy." I had never heard about the company Vietri, but soup tureens sell really well so I bought it. And besides, he was very cute.

Doing research on the Vietri Company was really interesting. They are the largest importer of Italian hand-crafted products for the "better specialty" (read, "expensive") market. On their website, they describe their story as a fairy tale about a mother inviting her two daughters on a long-planned trip to Italy. While there, they all fell in love with the hand-painted dinnerware at a hotel on the Amalfi coast. The women hired a driver to take them to the factory, and after three days of working with the owners, they left with a metal suitcase full of samples and big dreams. They chose the name "Vietri" for the company because it is the town where their first dinnerware pattern was made. The name Vietri also plays on the syllables in *"Tre Vita,"* which means "three lives."

This takes me back to a long-planned trip to Italy that also involved three lives (or, in my case, three generations). I was spending the winter semester of my junior year of college in Madrid, Spain. My brother was doing his senior year of high school in Barcelona. My mom and grandma decided to fly over with my sister and take us all to Italy for spring break. How exciting!

One of my favorite memories of this trip was the isle of Capri—which is, coincidentally, also on the Amalfi coast. I loved Capri and hope to return someday soon. I can still remember being rowed out in a little boat with my sister, brother and grandma into the blue grotto, one of the seven natural wonders of the world. You actually had to lie down in this tiny boat to get through the opening to the grotto. I just remember my grandmother laughing her great laugh. She was 72 years old at the time of that trip and was up for anything exciting.

I miss those times with her and all the adventures she included us in. Well, back to reality and my Vietri rabbit, which ended up selling for $79! Yikes. I always look for Vietri when I am out shopping now. What a life I have lived so far! The *dolce vita!*

#67 Timeshare

$5,000.⁰⁰

Paid

From: My friend's parents purchased new

Sunterra Marquis Villa Palm Springs, CA Timeshare-Golf!

Description:

New Super Low Reserve. I am selling this for a friend so please ask any questions early so that I can provide you with answers. Marquis Villa is located in Palm Springs. The timeshare term expires on 7/25/2045. There are currently 5829 points in the bank which must be used by 12/31/2004. At the beginning of 2005 you will start with a fresh 4000 point balance. 4,000 points are enough for one week in blue season. Annual maintenance is $232. Closing must be through an escrow service with all fees paid by the buyer (about $325) and a transfer fee ($125) will also be paid by the buyer. You can transfer these points to use at other locations.

Winning Bid: **$499.⁰⁰**

Ended: 12/15/04
History: 6 bids
Starting Bid: $49.99, $499 rsrv
Winner: Canada

Viewed
000325 X

The Story

My friend Kelly's parents Anne and Charles had a timeshare that they wanted to sell. Kelly asked me if I would help in exchange for some Pilates sessions. Sure! I am always up for selling different things on eBay. It is the best way to learn how (and how *not*) to do things.

For those of you who do not know what a timeshare is or have not been bombarded with timeshare solicitations by salesmen while on vacation, I will tell you. A timeshare is a condo, villa, cabin or hotel managed by a company that sells weekly occupancy plans to customers who expect to return year after year. Some timeshare companies allow you to bank your weeks or use them at other reciprocal properties.

My first experience with timeshares came when my mother started buying them (in bulk) in the 1990's. Remember, she is her mother's daughter, and before you knew it she had about eight weeks. Great for us—not so great for her. All of us kids got to go on all sorts of great vacations to Mexico and stay in amazing hotels for almost free! Unfortunately for her, the annual fees ended up being really expensive, and it was almost impossible to get the weeks she requested. She tried to sell her weeks, but never had any luck and ended up just giving them back to the company. We should have tried them on eBay!

Anyway, I did list Kelly's parent's timeshare on eBay. We tried a $1,495 reserve, but the bidding only got up to $525. The market was telling us that this timeshare wasn't worth much more than $500. When you sell a time-share, an escrow company should be involved to protect both the buyer and the seller. The escrow service costs $325, and there was also a $125 transfer fee, which a buyer would have to pay in addition to the purchase price. So out of the gate, any potential bidder was looking at $450.

After trying it at $1,495, the reality set in for Anne and Charles. They agreed to put it on eBay with a $499 reserve, and that is exactly what it sold for. What a relief! They just wanted to be out from under the annual maintenance fees of $232.

The couple who bought it were from Canada, and we started proceeding with the escrow company. It ended up taking about two months to close, and in the middle of the process we found out that the annual fees had increased to $540! The Canadian couple were livid and wanted to back out, thinking that we had lied. Both Anne and I wrote them saying that the fee increase was news to us also and if they wanted to back out of the deal that would be fine. They finally realized that we were telling the truth and decided to go forward with it anyway. When it was all over, I breathed a heavy sigh of relief and decided that I am perfectly happy selling just antiques and collectibles on eBay!

#68 AE Crowell Song Bird

$2.00
Paid
From: Thrift store

AE Elmer Crowell Signed Carved Original Song Bird RARE

Description:
This is a wonderful piece of early American Folk Art. Hand Carved by Master Carver A. E. Elmer Crowell. Signed with a rectangular mark. He first used this mark in 1928. I am guessing that this piece is 1930's to 1940's. The bird is 4" by 3 ⅞". He is one of the 25 song birds carved by Crowell. This darling little guy is a black capped chickadee. Incredible condition for its age. This auctions ends on Christmas Day. What a great present for yourself!

Winning Bid: **$2,051.00**

Ended: 12/25/04
History: 16 bids
Starting Bid: $99, $1995 reserve
Winner: MA

Viewed

000952 X

AE Crowell Song Bird   #68

The Story

It was the week before Christmas and all through Palm Desert, not a creature was stirring—not even a mouse. Please forgive me for that. I couldn't help myself. Anyway, it was Saturday morning and as usual my mom and I were out hitting the garage sales. There were not many. We had been to every one of the eight sales and all I had to show for myself was one tiny box in the back of her van. It was pitiful—the worst I had seen in about a year.

It was barely 10:00 AM and I asked my mom if she would mind going by my favorite thrift store, which opened at 10:00. She said, "Of course not," and off we went. When we walked in, right in front of me on my favorite shelf was a little bird. (This is the same shelf where I found the Venini Vase #77 from *The 100 Best*). The bird was carved wood and marked $2. When I turned him over, I found a signature hand-carved in the base. Who takes the time to sign anything by hand? I thought he must be pretty good. The fact that the signature said, "AE Crowell Maker, East Harwich, Mass," made him very appealing to me. "Maker" is an old-fashioned term. I carefully placed him in my shopping basket.

As I was checking out, I said to my mom, "This bird is really good. I am going to make sure that they wrap him very carefully." My mom looked at me like I was crazy and she said to me, "I wouldn't have given that bird a second look, much less picked him up and turned him over." When it comes to thrift store shopping, boy am I lucky that I take after my grandmother!

When we got home, I immediately got on eBay and did some research. Nothing had sold in the previous two weeks for "AE Crowell." Hmmmm, that could mean that the bird was really rare, or that it was not desirable. I next went to Google to do my research. I immediately found out a lot of great information. "AE Crowell" was Anthony Elmer Crowell. He was a master carver and one of the top duck decoy makers of all time. A goose decoy made by A. E. in 1917 recently fetched $684,500 at auction! I was jumping up and down and couldn't wait to call my mom.

I went back on eBay and found that one of his shore birds had sold in the past two weeks for $1,678.98. The reason it didn't turn up in my original search was because it was listed as Elmer Crowell and not "AE." I decided I wanted $2,000 for this little guy, so I listed it with a $1,995 reserve. I had many inquiries about this tiny bird. Almost one thousand people watched the auction. He sold for $2,051 on Christmas Day. Merry Christmas to me!!!!

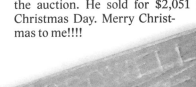

#69 Stephen Meader Books

$1.00 Paid

From: Thrift store and inheritance

Lumber Jack Stephen Meader Lumberjack 1934 FE Harcourt

Description:

Lumber Jack written by Stephen W. Meader, 1934 First edition (FE), Harcourt Brace NY. It is in OK condition. There are some tears on pages, pencil marks and some stains. It originally belonged to the Burbank CA High School Library.

Winning Bid:

$57.06/2

Ended: 12/30/04
History: 15 bids/2
Starting Bid: $9.99 each
Winner: PA and NC

Viewed

 **X**

Stephen Meader Books   #69

The Story

Houston came home from school the other day and told me, "You are not a prolific writer . . . yet." My son was only eight years old at the time and seemed to have a pretty good handle on what "prolific" meant, but I was a little vague on the definition. Of course, I had an idea, but I wasn't sure. I had to go and get my dictionary—oops, not really. I just used Google. It turns out prolific means "producing abundant works." I had thought that being prolific involved foretelling the future, but it really applies to authors who have written a lot of works.

These books that I sold on eBay were actually written by a prolific author, Stephen Meader. I had never heard of him until I pulled *Behind the Ranges* out of one of my boxes from the shop. I had it in my pile to sell on eBay but needed a few more things to make my 100 items for the week, so I headed out to my favorite thrift store. Amazingly enough, in their locked cabinet was another book by Stephen Meader entitled *Lumber Jack*. It was half-price day and this book that was marked $2 would only cost me $1. I bought it thinking that it would be great to put them both on eBay at the same time.

Books are a hard sell on eBay. Only the really rare ones, those in perfect condition, first editions, kitschy or strange books seem to sell. I have found that if a book doesn't sell with a $9.99 starting price, it is smart to put it right into my eBay store at a fixed price. I sell a lot of books from my eBay store by doing this.

Stephen Meader wrote nearly 50 novels celebrating the West and the American spirit of discovery. He averaged a novel per year. (I have been attempting to write a book a year also!) Most of his books were children's adventure novels and were considered inspirational for young men. When Stephen was twelve years old, his father quit his teaching position to become a lumberjack in New Hampshire.

Meader's *Lumber Jack,* based on his real-life experiences, sold for the most money of the two at $32. The other book that I had inherited, *Behind the Ranges,* also a first edition, sold for $25.06.

In doing research on Meader what struck me most was his son John's description of the way the author worked: "His powers of concentration were remarkable. He would sit in the living room writing while my brother, two sisters and I were in and out of the room playing with the dog, listening to the radio, or asking questions about homework." Boy, is that my life! Both kids were just in here asking me if they could type this while I dictated. Then they wanted to tell me all about their day and Indy needed to know how to spell "puppies." I finally just said, "Enough! I need some quiet time to finish this book!" They laughed and headed out to the living room. If they leave me alone long enough, maybe I can be a prolific writer someday!

#70 Moser Style Perfume

$0.⁰⁰ **Paid**
From: Inheritance

Miniature Antique Green Enameled Perfume Moser English

Description:
This perfume was in my grandmother's perfume collection. She was always trying to find the right top for it. She brought it over from England in the 1960's and it still has part of the container label on the base. 2 ½" by 2" and needs an atomizer top. Moser style and I think definitely English. Heavily enameled with gold and pink flowers.

Winning Bid:

$53.⁸⁰

Ended: 12/30/04
History: 6 bids
Starting Bid: $24.99
Winner: California

Viewed
 **X**

Moser Style Perfume #70

The Story

I knew that this perfume was not Moser, but I knew that I could get away with calling it "Moser style." Moser has become a generic term for heavy enameling on glass, much like Kleenex has become a generic term for tissue.

The Moser glass factory was named after Ludwig Moser (1822-1916) and was established in Bohemia (part of the modern-day Czech Republic) in 1857. Moser was best known for his heavily enameled designs and gold leaf work. Most pieces were not signed, but Moser realized early on that developing an easily recognizable style would serve as a trademark of sorts for his work. He had very wealthy customers who wanted to show off their expensive glass in a discreet manner, and making sure it was recognizable as Moser glass would make this possible. Moser achieved a distinctive style by using applied glass acorns and enameled glass insects, grapes and birds. Moser considered the quality of his glass to be of the utmost importance, and he made sure that any inferior glass produced in his factory was destroyed. As a result, pieces of Moser produced after 1893 (when they began blowing their own glass) will never have a bubble or any other internal flaws. These antique Moser pieces can bring in thousands of dollars. Moser is still in business today.

This piece was from my grandmother's perfume collection and it had heavy gold leaf but not heavy expensive enamel. People say that once you have held a real piece of Moser, you will forever be spoiled. My grandmother did have real pieces of Moser and I have to admit that they were amazing. She would show us a piece from one of her cabinets and tell us the story of where she bought it. Most of her Moser came from England and she was extremely proud of those pieces.

She traveled to Europe a lot in the 1960's. She often borrowed money from her father, George Sussex, to buy stock for the shop. Her father (as you know) was a banker from way back and he made her put everything in writing. She would borrow $10,000 or $15,000 for each trip and bring back a container full of antiques. This was long before everyone started doing this. She would pay him back within months, if not weeks. It is so nice to have a family member who believes in you enough to loan you money. Luckily, even without my grandma, I still have several of these around!

Heads Both Banks

—Photo by Simmer.
GEORGE SUSSEX, Jr., president of the Cashmere State Bank, who will head the consolidated bank.

However, this was a darling perfume and perfume collectors are a serious bunch. I knew that it should bring at least $24.99, so that is where I started the auction. I was very happy when it sold for $53.80 and went to Paradise, California. Owning a Moser piece is like owning a little piece of paradise.

#71 Bakelite Stapler

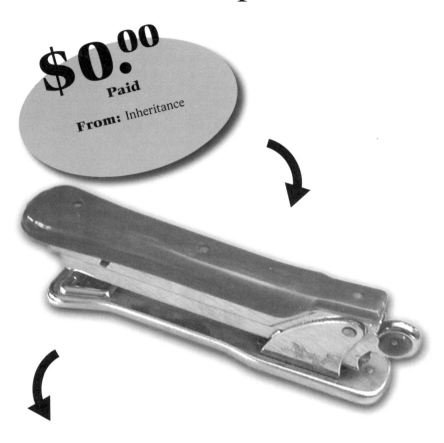

$0.00 Paid

From: Inheritance

Ace Liner Vintage Apple Green Bakelite Stapler Mottled

Description:
This stapler is signed "Ace Liner." It is a great green apple color. Mottled. Vintage model #502. 7 ½". In good condition. Needs cleaning. I didn't test it with staples. I believe that it is bakelite.

Winning Bid: **$30.00**

Ended: 1/4/05
History: 8 bids
Starting Bid: $9.99
Winner: Texas

Viewed

000103 X

Bakelite Stapler #71

The Story

When I was in sixth grade, we moved to Bellingham, Washington. My mom and dad had grown up there but left after getting married. They had moved all around North America. When I was born, we were living in Bloomington, Indiana. From there, my mom and dad moved us to Monmouth, Oregon, Edmonton, Alberta (Canada), and finally Olympia, Washington. They were getting closer and closer to their hometown. Finally, my dad took a job with the Bellingham school district and my mom was pleased to be back near her folks.

My mom and dad decided to build an awesome house in the Edgemoor section of Bellingham. It is right on the ocean and really nice. Building the house was going to take about a year, so we moved into the upstairs apartment at my grandma's.

To get to school at Fairhaven Middle School, which was on the other side of town, I had to ride the city bus by myself. It took 40 minutes each way, and I remember those rides as rather scary and lonely. I had just left all my friends in Olympia and had to start middle school in a new town where I knew no one. It was a hard year. I will try my best never to move my kids during such a critical transition.

However, there was a bright side to that year. I could go down the stairs anytime and visit, work or just hang out with my grandma. One of my monthly jobs was to pay her bills. I received $5 a week for doing this. Wouldn't it be great to have someone pay all your bills for $5 a week? She had a lot of bills because of the business, and I learned quickly how to take a discount for early payment, record all the data in her check register, and balance a checkbook.

I used to sit at her big desk to pay the bills. Her desk was made out of two drawer sections with a big oak door on the top. It is the same desk I used many years later when I ran the store for her. On the desktop was this green bakelite stapler. Who knew that many years later, I would inherit it in one of my boxes and sell it on eBay?

The stapler was signed "Ace Liner." I started to do some research on staplers in general. If you can believe it, there are many people who collect them (if you haven't realized it yet, there is a collector for everything!). Staplers have quite a history. Legend has it that the first stapler was developed during the 1700's for the exclusive use of King Louis XV of France. Some historians claim that his staples were made of gold. Wow! The first American stapler patent was awarded to George McGill in 1879.

The stapler that I sold was probably from the 1950's and really neat with its bakelite top. I was so happy when it sold for $30! From my grandma's desktop to my box in California to Sugarland, Texas. Funny how collectors make the world go round!

#72   Rhinestone Bracelets

$0.⁰⁰ Paid

From: Inheritance

Bakelite Vintage Green Bangle Bracelet Clear Rhinestones

Description:
This is a great bracelet. My grandmother collected these vintage bakelite/celluloid bracelets with rhinestones. We have four different ones up for auction this week. I have included a picture of all four. Your are only bidding on ONE bracelet/bangle. This one is an unusual green with clear or white rhinestones bezel set and indented. ⅜" by 3". In excellent condition. 1930's or so.

Winning Bid: **$126.⁰⁷/4**

Ended: 1/5/05
History: 18 bids/4
Starting Bids: $24.99/3, $9.99/1
Winner: Denmark, Washington DC

Viewed

000337 X

Rhinestone Bracelets #72

The Story

When my grandmother got older, she moved from her bedroom in the old house/shop (the "middle bedroom") into a bedroom in the new addition. It was super tiny. The reason for this was because the city of Bellingham wouldn't zone the new addition as retail space. So she made the kitchen and bedroom super small in case they changed their mind and she could move the shop from the old house into the new quarters. Well, a girl can hope, can't she? It never happened.

On a shelf right above her bed she kept a silk box about the size of a shoebox. Inside were all her rhinestone bangles. She loved these bracelets and would pick them up during her travels. She had about 30 of them and my grandma and I had so much fun playing with them. I inherited four of them and decided to sell them on eBay so that I would have some cash for an excursion I had planned.

I was getting ready to go into LA for a big party. My good friend Dean Factor was turning 40 and his wife Shannon was throwing the best party. They had rented out an entire restaurant in Westwood (EuroChow) and the theme was the 1980's. I had spent several weeks scouring thrift stores looking for outfits for Peter and myself. I found him a Miami Vice-style

jacket with stripes and some linen pants. If you can believe it, I still had some 1980's outfits in my closet (of course you can—I never throw anything away). I had black stretch pants, furry cowboy boots and a Prince-style long blazer. We were ready!

We had so much fun—the party was a blast. There were impersonators for Prince, Madonna, Boy George and Michael Jackson. The music they played was so awesome. We were dancing to some of our favorite 80's hits—"Melt With You," "Tainted Love," and "I Love Rock and Roll." And while this mayhem and madness was going on, I made over $125 on eBay with these bangles.

"Bangle" is a great word to use for a bracelet when you are selling on eBay. A bangle is a rigid bracelet that slips over the hand. It is not flexible. The original word was Indian, and meant a ring of colored glass worn on the wrist by women

I started all four auctions at $24.99. Three of the bangles sold for more than that and went to Denmark. I had to relist one at $9.99, and that bangle eventually sold for $13.97. Hey, weren't the Bangles an all-girl band from the 1980's? I think I danced to their song "Manic Monday" that weekend!

#73 Hudson Pewter Walli Girl

$0.00 Paid
From: Inheritance

Hudson Pewter USA 063 Walli Ortman Little Girl Vintage

Description:
This adorable little girl is signed "Hudson Pewter USA" and "063" on the base. 1 ⅝" by 2 ½". "Walli" is written on the back side. A little girl looking at yellow mushrooms. In great shape. These are from the "Littles" series also known as the "Little Wallis." Darling and very 1960's to 1970's.

Winning Bid:

$41.50

Ended: 1/21/05
History: 10 bids
Starting Bid: $9.99
Winner: Illinois

Viewed
 **X**

Hudson Pewter Walli Girl #73

The Story

I remember putting this piece out for more than one yard sale. It was priced in masking tape at 50 cents and somehow found its way to me. We used to have the most amazing yard sales at the shop. We called them "The World's Greatest Yard Sale" and I would send out postcard invitations to our local mailing list of 2,000 people. The postcard would show my grandmother's head on a cartoon body standing on top of the world.

My grandmother and I would spend several weeks prior to the sale in the basement pricing and pricing and pricing. That seemed to be all we ever did at the shop—price and price. There was an overwhelming amount of merchandise that never actually made it to the shop because we just couldn't price it all. Back then, before eBay, we had to come up with prices using the PFA (pull from air) technique. "PFA" was one of my grandmother's favorite phrases. PFA pricing was tough. You always worried that you were pricing too high—or worse yet, too low. Sometimes when my grandmother and I were pricing, we would say, "OK, 1-2-3 name the price!" It was fun, and more often than not, we would both blurt out the exact same price. And then we would both laugh. We got a kick out of the fact that we were so similar!

My grandma had a funny standard for her prices and I guess it just developed from 50 years of being in business. Most prices ended in .50. The pricing scale went .50, 1.50, 2.50, 3.50, 4.50, 5.00, 6.50, 7.50, 8.50, 9.50, 10.00, 11.50, 12.50, 13.50, 14.50, 15.00, 16.50, 17.50, 18.50, 19.50, 20.00, 21.50. It was strange, but in my grandma's system, you could never do a multiple of five with a .50. Anyway, many times when we would be pricing, we would tend to favor one price point for a whole day. I would say to my grandma, "Boy, we are sure on a $19.50 kick today. Maybe we should mix it up?" The next time we named a price, we would both say, "$22.50" or "$25" just to break our streak, and then we would laugh. Let me tell you, anything to break the monotony.

Now, with eBay, I can let the world-wide marketplace price for me. Letting the market determine the price is a huge time saver, and more often than not, I get way more money than I would have if I had set a price on my own.

This little figurine was really cute and I was lucky that it hadn't sold for only 50 cents. I knew it was from the 1970's and it was signed with "Hudson Pewter" and "Walli Ortman." I couldn't find out much about the artist except that she was a mother who modeled these figures from memories of her girls, and her figurines are super-collectible. Most have a blank face and are very stylized, very mid-century modern. It turned out that I didn't need to know any more about her because several eBay bidders already did. They took the figurine's price from $9.99 to $41.50 for me! Funny, it was a price approved by my grandmother in her pricing scale!

#74 Antique Doll Body

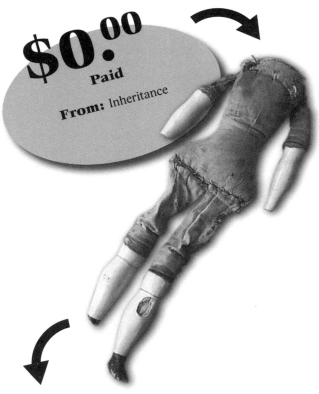

$0.00 Paid

From: Inheritance

Antique China Doll Body Sawdust 1800's As Is Arms Feet

Description:
This is the neatest doll body, but it needs some TLC. I hope we find someone to fix her up! She is from about 1800 to 1880, and is still really sweet even with her problems. Her hands and one boot are broken off. There is a hole in the leg with the boot. 10 ¾" by 3 ¼" and some holes in the burlap/muslin fabric. Some of the sawdust is coming out. A great piece of early Americana.

Winning Bid:

$29.77

Ended: 1/22/05
History: 6 bids
Starting Bid: $9.99
Winner: Connecticut

Viewed
 X

Antique Doll Body #74

The Story

Doesn't this just go to show you that you can sell ANYTHING on eBay? I'm not kidding. This doll body is something that 99.9% of the world would throw away, and yet I got almost $30 for it!

The reason my grandmother kept this doll for so many years was because she was a rescuer. She always wanted to fix things that were broken. She wanted to match the missing stopper to the empty perfume bottle, make a lamp out of a box of parts, and design beautiful jewelry from assorted beads and stones. And she DID create these things. Her life was full of creativity, which is one reason she was so happy. I believe that when people are creating (in any medium), they are at their best.

My grandmother's mother, Maybelle, was a very talented painter. She passed away when my grandmother was only eighteen months old. It was very painful for my grandmother to grow up without a mother. She would often talk about her mom and wonder "what if." My grandma would say, "My mother was a very talented artist. I didn't inherit any of her ability." The funny thing was, she did. My grandmother was just blessed with artistic talents that were used in an unconventional way. She wasn't a good painter, it's true—but she was a wonderful designer.

This doll body would have been made for a china doll head. China dolls were manufactured, mostly in Germany, from 1830 until about 1930.

Millions of dolls were produced during this period; every little girl either had a china doll or dreamed of having a china doll.

A china doll's head is glazed bisque with a shiny finish; it ends at the shoulder plate. They came in every size, from under 2" to over 30". Most were not signed. Their bodies were either cloth or leather, and sometimes (like my doll) they had glazed lower arms and legs.

This doll body must have had a lot of love over the years to be this worn out! Kat, the incredible doll collector who bought it, tells me that this doll was from the Civil War-era, a fact that is revealed in its flat feet. After 1870, dolls had fatter calves and a heeled boot. How neat!

Kat has not used the body yet and it rests in one of her carefully labeled drawers of antique doll parts and bodies. "Sort of like the morgue on CSI!" she says. She loves the china dolls the most because (as she writes), "They

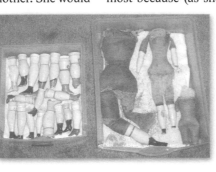

are so mysterious and serene. Why would anyone make a doll out of something so fragile, especially for a small child?" Kat emailed me a photo of her doll "catacombs" and our doll body is on the right. Kat is hoping some day to have the right head for the body. She also writes, "You can see the piles of parts I have—they'll probably outlive me!" My grandmother used to say the same thing about all her stuff!

#75 Heath Buffet Bowl

$1.00 Paid

From: Garage sale

Heath Opaque White CA Pottery Buffet Serving Bowl RARE

Description:
Heath Buffet bowl is style #302. It has a sand rim—also known as the rim shape. 10 ½" by 1 ¾" and very hard to find. California pottery. In excellent condition. No chips, no cracks, no crazing. We have a lot of wonderful dinnerware up for sale this week.

Winning Bid:

$75.98

Ended: 1/25/05
History: 12 bids
Starting Bid: $9.99
Winner: Montana

Viewed

000153 X

Heath Buffet Bowl #75

The Story

I love dinnerware. I don't know why. For some reason it fascinates me and I am always amazed to see how well it sells on eBay. So I was very happy when I stumbled across a garage sale with hundreds of dinnerware singles. The woman was a tabletop sales rep and had literally one each of 400 different plates, cups and saucers, and serving pieces. The only pieces that matched were the cups and their saucers.

She wanted $1 for each piece, so I started making a pile of what I wanted. After about ten minutes, I said, "This is ridiculous. How much for all of it?" She and her husband were shocked, but we struck a deal. I think I ended up paying about $150 and carted box after box after box into my mom's minivan.

One of the nicest pieces was this Heath California pottery serving bowl. I have sold Heath pottery before and knew that it went well on eBay, so I put this piece on immediately.

Heath Ceramics was started in Sausalito, CA, in 1948 by Edith Heath. She had staged a one-woman ceramic show in San Francisco that ended with her pieces being picked up for sale at Gumps (a very high end store). Funny, but around the same time, 1950, Cheryl Leaf Antiques and Gifts was started in Bellingham, Washington, by my grandmother.

Edith's designs were an instant success, perhaps because they were very distinctive. Her style was very avant-garde at the time, and very mid-century modern. Her company is still in business today and Edith Heath is known as a pioneer for her techniques and finishes.

My grandmother was also a pioneer in the antiques industry. In 1950, not many women were in business, and antiques stores were rare. My grandmother took her business to the next level by importing from England in the 1960's, exploding the collector's plate business in the 1970's and hitting the road for antiques shows in the 1980's. She had such an entrepreneurial spirit.

Edith Heath passed away in December of 2005 at the age of 94. My grandmother would have been 93 at the time of Edith's death if she had lived. I think that these women were very similar. Both were members of a generation whose values were influenced by the Depression, when resources were scarce. Edith used that as inspiration for her glazes and for her sleek, simple designs. My grandmother used the Depression as inspiration for saving, recycling and creating beautiful items from just bits and pieces. Both women were pioneers in their field and both lived their lives with a passion for their work.

This wonderful piece of Heath pottery ended up selling for $75.98 on what would have been my grandmother's 93rd birthday. Strange, isn't it?

#76 Buick Hood Ornament

$0.⁵⁰
Paid
From: Garage sale

Car Part Medallion Hood Ornament Buick Metal Tri Shield

Description:

This car medallion is about 2 ¼" round. No metal pins on the back side. Must have been glued on. Red, white and blue. Marked on the back with "12030" and "1." In good to very good condition. Needs cleaning. What model and what year? 1959, I am guessing. We have a few vintage car medallions, logos and decals up for sale this week.

Winning Bid:

$15.⁵⁰

Ended: 1/30/05
History: 7 bids
Starting Bid: $9.99
Winner: Massachusetts

Viewed

000040 X

Buick Hood Ornament #76

The Story

My first car was a 1964 green VW Bug—license ILY338. My awesome mom gave me $500 on my 16th birthday and I earned the rest to buy it for $800. It was so cute! After I drove the VW, it passed on to my brother and eventually to my sister and finally it was sold. I miss that car!

I had heard such amazing success stories of people selling old car parts (doors, seats, insignias, hood ornaments, etc.) on eBay that I wanted to try some. I found a few logos and insignias at a garage sale and paid only 50 cents for this one. I had no idea what car or manufacturer it belonged to.

I got it home and showed it to my brother (who was visiting) and my eight-year-old son. Before my brother could even respond, Houston jumped in, saying, "That is like the one on daddy's car—it's a Buick." I said, "Get out. Are you for real?" Lee backed Houston up. Yes, it was a Buick hood ornament. I guess it must be a guy thing. I can tell you what kind of a purse that girl over there is carrying but I couldn't tell you what kind of car this hood ornament came from.

With that knowledge (from an eight-year-old, mind you) I did a little research. David Dunbar Buick, a Scotsman, founded Buick in 1903. David had been born in Scotland in 1854 and brought to the United States when he was two. He was a successful businessman in Detroit when he turned his attention to gasoline engines in the late 1890's. Since then, Buick has had a long and notable career.

The history of the emblem is very interesting.

In the mid 1930's, a Buick researcher working in the Detroit public library found an 1851 Burke's Heraldry book that contained a description (without a picture) of the Scottish Buick (Buik) family's ancestral arms. The book described it as a red shield with a checkered silver and light blue diagonal line, an antlered deer head with a jagged neckline, and a gold cross.

The first shield (drawn to these specifications) was used on cars in 1937, and over the years it was slightly modified until 1959, when it was completely overhauled. Instead of one shield, it now had three shields (or a tri-shield), one for each of the three car models being produced that year: the LeSabre, Invicta and Electra. The colors and symbols were retained. How cool is that? It was fun to look closer at my shield and see the antlered deer and the cross. My shield was the tri-shield variety!

The emblem was changed again in 1975 and has been completely modernized today. There is no more deer's head or cross. I can see why this would be such a collectible piece. It ended up selling for $15.50—pretty great for a 50-cent investment—and now I know what kind of car my ex-husband drives. Do I really need to know that?

#77 Dansk Flatware

$20.00 Paid

From: Garage sale

Dansk Variation IV Finland 5 Pc Place Setting Stainless

Description:

This five-piece place setting is all signed Dansk Finland. You get a table (place) spoon, tea spoon, dinner fork, salad fork, and dinner knife. Quite a hard-to-find pattern. These 5 pieces sell for $178.00 on a popular china replacement site. We have a lot of pieces up for sale this week in separate auctions. Variation IV 4 Stainless with NO Black Accent. It has the usual estate wear and could use a cleaning but still in very good condition. IHQ which means it was designed by Jens Quistgaard.

Winning Bid: **$204.76/13**

Ended: 1/30/05
History: 30 bids/13
Starting Bid: $9.99 each
Winner: MA, NM, NY

Viewed

000229 X

Dansk Flatware #77

The Story

I found this set at a garage sale in Rancho Mirage, and the sellers wanted $20 for the bunch. I turned a piece over and saw "Dansk Finland," and quickly decided to buy it. When I got home and pulled up Replacements. com, I was shocked to read the name of the pattern. "Variation IV." What kind of a name for flatware is that? Oh, well, it was Dansk and it was designed by Jens Quistgaard. I guess he is famous enough to call it whatever he wants.

When I got on eBay and did my research for this pattern, I found that it sold quite well. I also noticed something new during this research. The full five-piece place settings typically sold better than listings that only contained multiple like items (such as two teaspoons or three knives). Because of this, I tried listing a full place setting for the first time instead of my usual two spoons, two forks and so on.

Just what comes in a full five-piece place setting, and how do you set a table with flatware anyway? You know, I was lucky. My grandmother (of course) was a stickler for this kind of thing, and I learned early on how to set a table. It sure came in handy later when I was going to fancy lunches and dinners in my sorority. I didn't feel like a complete idiot—at least for the majority of the time—although I do remember being at a fancy restaurant (on a date) when a sorbet was served between courses.

"Why are we getting dessert now?" I asked. My date informed me that the sorbet was intended to cleanse the palate. Oops—I still have a lot to learn.

Back to the flatware...when you set a table, you are supposed to place the silver that will be used for the first course on the outside, the silver for the second course inside that, and so on in toward the plate, with forks to the left of the plate and knives and spoons to the right. A standard five-piece place setting consists of a dinner fork, salad fork, tablespoon, teaspoon and dinner knife.

I listed a single five-piece place setting as a test. The five-piece set sold for $49, and when broken up and sold in smaller lots, the same pieces brought in only $41.37. So for this pattern, the five-piece setting was the way to go. As a result of this auction, I have changed my flatware strategy. I now make all the five-piece settings that I can first, and then sell whatever is left over in lots of two, three, or four. See, I learn something new every day, too!

Altogether, the items in these thirteen auctions sold for over $200, so I was happy. As my grandmother would say, "As long as you made your 10%." Try a 900% return on this one!

#78 Fabrik Dinner Set

$20.⁰⁰ **Paid**
From: Garage sale

Fabrik Seattle WA Ptarmigan 2 Dinner Plates Stoneware

Description:

These dinner plates are 10 ⅞". Slight wear, need cleaning. No chips, no cracks. In very good to excellent condition. One of the plates has a slight nick/indentation that is under the glaze—so done in the making. Not really worth mentioning but we try to be overly critical. We have a lot of this pattern up for sale this week. Fabrik signs its wares with a stylized "F." Their items are very mid-century modern and Eames era in look and appeal. This pattern is Ptarmigan (named after a bird) and is a cream with brown flecked stoneware—much like oatmeal. Fabrik was handmade in Seattle, WA.

Winning Bid: $652.⁰¹/18

Ended: 1/30/05
History: 83 bids/18
Starting Bid: $9.99 each
Winner: MD, AZ, CA, WI

Viewed
000577 X

Fabrik Dinner Set #78

The Story

I was at the same garage sale where I bought the Dansk flatware. There was a box of strange-looking dinnerware on the ground. I had never seen anything like it and when I turned it over, there was a very bizarre looking "F" on the back side. The sellers wanted $20 for the box.

I knew that these people had nice things because of the Dansk flatware. So I asked them, "What do you know about these dishes?" The lady told me that they were made by a Seattle, Washington company named Fabrik. Funny, I had grown up 90 miles north of Seattle and had never heard of it. I bought the dishes and had the lady write down "Fabrik" on a piece of paper. I would never remember that name by the time I got home.

My favorite thing to do when I have unloaded my mom's minivan after a Saturday of saling is to jump on my computer. The research is so fun! I can't wait to see if I have found anything great. I really wanted to be a detective when I was growing up—I loved the book *Harriet the Spy*. In sixth grade, Melanie Souve and I used to run around peeking in people's houses. Can you believe we are still friends? I love mysteries and gathering clues. Being an antiques dealer involves solving multiple mysteries every day, and I really enjoy discovering the history of each company or artist. It really is a perfect job for me.

Anyway, I found that Fabrik was listed on the Replacements web site and that the name of my pattern was "Ptarmigan." A ptarmigan is a small bird that is white in winter and brown in summer—much like the speckling on my plates.

Replacements had ZERO pieces for sale. Such a great sign!

I couldn't find out very much about the company. It appears that Fabrik dinnerware was originally hand-thrown by Jim McBride in Seattle back in the 1970's. Later pieces were pressed. The work was very distinctive with wide rims that slanted outward to form handles. Glazing was simple and the colors were mainly earth tones. The factory thrived for a number of years, but it gradually faded away or went bankrupt.

It turns out that Fabrik has quite a loyal following. The action on these eighteen auctions was insane! People were going nuts for these pieces. Two dinner plates ended up selling for $119.49. One lady who didn't win them emailed after the auction frenzy to remark that, "At least if I didn't win them, the person who did had to pay through the nose!" Where did that expression come from? Being the amateur detective that I am, I can tell you. Apparently there was a "nose tax" levied upon the Irish by the Danes in the ninth century. Those who did not pay had their noses slit. Creepy!

All told, I received over $650 for the set on eBay. And what is really strange is that none of the buyers were from Washington State. What a wonderful world!

#79 Perrier Jouët Bottle

$3.

$3.³³ Paid

From: Garage sale

Perrier Jouët Champagne Epernay 1988 Display BIG Bottle

Description:

This is such a great piece. Made for display in restaurants and bars, it is larger than a normal champagne bottle. 15 ½" by 4 ½". There is nothing on the inside. Says "1988 Epernay" and "Cuvee Belle Époque." The bottle is hand-painted and the foil is still intact at the top. What a great piece! In very good to excellent condition.

Winning Bid:

$29.⁹⁸

Ended: 1/30/05
History: 7 bids
Starting Bid: $9.99
Winner: New York

Viewed

000107 X

Perrier Jouët Bottle #79

The Story

On the ground in someone's driveway were three huge display bottles of wine and champagne. They must have been from a bar or restaurant. The guy only wanted $10 for all three, so I lugged them home.

I love Perrier Jouët champagne. I bought a bottle once in an expensive Paris restaurant—on that same trip to France during which I actually drank coffee with my friends Juliette and Vicki. I didn't really buy the champagne, though—my mom did, since I used her charge card, and boy was she mad when I saw her again. I think it cost $100. I was in deep trouble. But guess who bailed me out? You guessed it—my grandmother.

The Perrier Jouët company history is awesome. Its web site begins, "Like all the best stories, this one starts with a wedding, and this love match forged the destiny of a great Champagne House." I have to admit I was very intrigued and couldn't wait to learn more. In 1811, Pierre Nicolas-Marie Perrier married Adele Jouët (Adelle is my middle name, by the way), and they set up a champagne trading house in the French town of Epernay. It was a huge success, and in 1902 they hired master glassmaker Emile Gallé to decorate a magnum bottle for the house's quality vintage. It was a true work of art, combining a design of white anemones and enameled roses circled with gold.

This amazing piece lay forgotten in the Perrier cellars for almost sixty years and was never marketed. In 1964, the magnum was discovered, and plans to launch a "Belle Époque" vintage cuvee were developed with the bottle as the cornerstone. In 1969, it was unveiled—and this amazing example of Art Nouveau design still adorns bottles to this day. Wow! What a history.

My grandmother loved the artistry of Emil Gallé and collected his work. She had several pieces, but her favorite was a large red cameo vase that she bought from famed antiques dealer Lillian Nassau during a trip to New York City in 1963. She paid $100 for the piece and it was one of her prized possessions. Can you believe that twenty years later, a regular-sized bottle of real champagne could cost as much as my grandmother's treasured piece of original art?

But back to the display bottle of Perriet Jouët (which, as I noted in the auction description, contained no actual liquid.) I used a title that emphasized the "display piece" angle for this bottle and put it up on eBay. I was very happy when it sold for almost $30—about ten times what I paid for it, and about one-third the price I paid for that real bottle of Perrier Jouët champagne in Paris. Oops, excuse me. . . what my mom paid. . . oops, excuse me. . . what my grandma paid!

#80 Art Deco Green Lamp

$0.⁵⁰ Paid

From: Thrift store

Art Deco Eames Era California Pottery Green Lamp Bauer?

Description:

Art Deco Lamp. This is the neatest lamp—I wish it were signed. It looks like California pottery to me and if anyone knows the maker we would love to know. A great green color and a great shape. No chips no cracks. The pottery portion is 7 ¾" tall and 5" by 3". I would guess 1930's to 1950's.

Winning Bid:

$53.⁰⁰

Ended: 1/31/05
History: 6 bids
Starting Bid: $9.99
Winner: California

Viewed
 X

Art Deco Green Lamp #80

The Story

I couldn't believe it when I saw this awesome art deco-style lamp in my favorite thrift store priced at only 50 cents. I put it in my basket right away. There were no maker's marks on it, but that was okay. Few lamps were ever marked or signed. The color was a great vibrant lime green and just screamed, "California pottery." The Art Deco era (1910 to 1930) is known for a simplified style that used geometric shapes and intense colors.

I have done really well with lamps on eBay. I think this is because many shoppers overlook them. After I think I am done at a sale, I make myself take one last look around, focusing on the ceiling fixtures, floor and table lamps. These things are easy to overlook because they often seem to be part of the display, rather than merchandise. I am often amazed at what I missed on my first glance.

I understand why lamps sell so well on eBay. They are decorative items that are relatively cheap to ship—$25 to $45—unlike larger pieces of furniture, which may cost more to ship than to buy. A lamp also brightens up any room and makes it cheery. You can never have too much light in a room.

I once got caught up in a lamp-buying frenzy. I can't believe that I am admitting this, but yes, I too shop on eBay, and sometimes I let my emotions do my bidding. I was searching for the perfect lamp and came across one that had pansies all over it—in my color scheme. It had been photographed beautifully, so that it looked like the design was done in pottery. I decided I had to have that lamp. Apparently, so did another eBay bidder. We got into a huge bidding war and I ended up paying $82.77 for a lamp that should have cost $25!

Anyway, when the lamp arrived, it looked nothing like the photo. What I had thought was a pottery design turned out to be a pattern made with shellacked stickers. I still use the lamp because it is cute, but every time I walk by it, I am reminded to do my due diligence before and during bidding.

The darling unmarked lamp that I bought for 50 cents ended up getting six bids and selling for $53! It went to Santa Cruz, California, a perfect home for a lamp that reminded me of the ocean and California!

When packing a lamp to ship, remember to take the harp off so that it can fit more compactly inside the box. The harp is the metal part that holds up the shade. Maureen was shipping a lamp for me last week and I hadn't told her this trick. She ended up spending an hour to make a box big enough to accommodate the extra eight inches that the harp added. She was really mad at me for not telling her that the harp was removable! I should be mad at myself also, because I paid her for that extra hour!

#81 Mannequin Hand

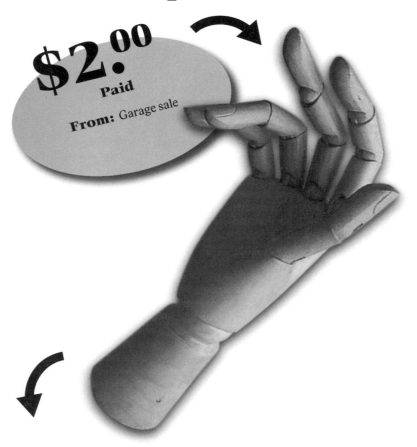

$2.⁰⁰ Paid

From: Garage sale

Wooden Jointed Mannequin Hand Authentic Handmade COOL!

Description:
Wooden mannequin hand. Made in China for Authentic Models, also marked "Handmade." Very cool. It is jointed everywhere and in great shape. 10 ¼" by 3 ½". A great piece.

Winning Bid: **$38.¹³**

Ended: 1/31/05
History: 13 bids
Starting Bid: $9.99
Winner: Texas

Viewed
 **X**

Mannequin Hand #81

The Story

This was such a neat item that when I saw it at a garage sale, I quickly picked it up. Even though it was made of jointed wood, it looked almost real. I liked the fact that the fingers were movable and could be posed in different positions. It was just creepy and unique enough to sell well on eBay.

I knew that there are collectors for life-size mannequins and head mannequins. A mannequin is a three-dimensional representation of the human form. It can be somewhat idealized and stylized for purposes of displaying apparel. Mannequins vary in size and proportions depending upon type, age group, manufacturer and current fashion look.

I didn't even know that there was

to be interviewed on a show with Jim "Griff" Griffin and his co-host Lee Mirabal. Griff is "The eBay Spokesperson," and he's a really great guy.

During one of our interviews, we got onto the subject of what NOT to show in photographs. I said, "Never model clothing or photograph shoes on your own feet. People just don't want to see that. It is unsanitary, too personal, and introduces the idea that the item of clothing is 'used,' regardless of its actual condition. It is kind of creepy." He laughed, and asked about sellers displaying jewelry on their hands. We both agreed that this was also a big no-no. We then discussed the "Seinfeld" episode where George was going to become a hand model.

such a thing as a hand mannequin. I suppose it would be used by jewelry manufacturers or designers to display their work. I wouldn't think that there would be a huge demand for these. I also didn't think that there would have been many of them made.

It was about the time I found this item that I had decided to advertise on eBay Radio. eBay Radio is played every Tuesday on the Internet, and it has some really great ad rates. As part of the advertising package, I was going

Unless you have hands as pretty as George Costanza's, you should not be modeling jewelry.

Someone who sells rings or bracelets on eBay may have purchased this wooden hand. I just don't know. But it received a lot of bids and ended up selling for almost $40. I loved "Seinfeld" because it was a show about nothing. Much like eBay, a web site where you make money out of almost nothing.

#82 Belleek Honey Bee Pot

$0.⁰⁰
Paid

From: Friend inherited

Belleek Honey Bee Pot Jar Shamrocks RARE Darling Gold

Description:
Belleek Honey Bee Pot Jar is signed with the gold mark style 44 sticker on the base. 4" by 4 ¾". Handle is a branch. Decorated with bees and shamrocks. Summer Briar Kylemore. In excellent condition; needs cleaning. No chips, no cracks, no crazing. Gold Mark.

Winning Bid:

$61.⁰⁰

Ended: 2/4/05
History: 17 bids
Starting Bid: $9.99
Winner: Pennsylvania

Viewed
 **X**

Belleek Honey Bee Pot #82

The Story

During my college semester in Spain, I met many good friends. One of them, John Lienhard, had the most incredible parents. Pat and Jerry lived in Glendale, and quickly became like second parents to me. They had a vacation home in Palm Desert, and I spent many weekends escaping from LA at their place. In 1988, they both retired to Palm Desert.

Whenever we left Los Angeles to drive out to the desert, my blood pressure would lower immediately and I would start to feel calm and relaxed. It was because of all these good memories that when I decided to move back to California, Palm Desert was my choice.

I asked Pat to read at my wedding. She did a wonderful job. She and Jerry came to Bellingham for the entire four-day ceremony, which included a golf tournament, a rehearsal dinner at the Yacht Club, a boat tour of the San Juan Islands, and a wedding shower at my mom's house. Saturday was the actual wedding, complete with a horse-drawn carriage. Sunday, there was a brunch at the Cliffhouse restaurant. It was quite the extravaganza, and people are still talking about it today. Too bad the marriage wasn't as good as the party.

Four years before I moved to Palm Desert, Pat passed away from cancer. I flew down for the funeral; it was extremely sad. I still miss her. This Belleek honey jar belonged to her, and the family asked me to sell it for them. I was happy to do it.

Pat was Irish through and through. She loved Notre Dame and Belleek.

The history of the Belleek Company is fascinating. In 1849, John Caldwell Bloomfield inherited the Castle Caldwell estate from his father, which encompassed the city of Belleek. John was very concerned about his tenants after the potato famine, so he started searching for a way to employ them. An amateur mineralogist, he ordered a geological survey of the land. He was thrilled to find that it had the raw materials necessary to make pottery—feldspar, kaolin, flint, clay and shale.

In 1858, the building of the factory began. Bloomfield lured fourteen designers from England's Stoke-on-Trent area with high wages. The rest is history. The company is still in operation today, with over 600 employees.

There are a lot of collectors for Honey Bee Pots, which is another reason this auction went so high. Whenever I see a honey pot, I always buy it. Of the fifteen or so that I have put up for auction over the years, all have sold! I don't have any left over in my eBay store.

I miss Patricia Lienhard, especially now that I live in her town. I often think how fun it would be to meet her for lunch or dinner. I know that she would have used her magic networking skills to set me up with all sorts of friends and business contacts. That is what she loved to do—connect people with other people. Kind of like what eBay does. Connecting buyers with sellers.

#83   12 Days of Christmas Bells

$5.^**00**
Paid
From: Garage sale

12 Days of Christmas Bell MIB #1 Partridge in Pear Tree

Description:

Twelve Days of Christmas Bell mint in box. #1 Partridge in Pear Tree. We have the whole set of 12 up for auction this week, so please check out our other auctions. These are the Twelve Days of Christmas Bells from Breckenridge Holidays. 1992 Mercuries USA. They come in the original boxes and are bisque. They measure 6 ½" tall by 2 ⅝" wide. They need cleaning. There are some scratches (typical of bisque ware) and some wear to the lettering.

Winning Bid: **$186.**^**00**/**12**

Ended: 2/11/05
History: 53 bids/12
Starting Bid: $1.99
Winner: Texas

Viewed
000195 **X**

12 Days of Christmas Bells #83

The Story

It was after Christmas, and these bells were in a box on the ground at a garage sale. They had been priced at $10 for the box, but there had been no takers. The lady having the sale saw me looking at them and said, "How about $5?" Sold. I have been noticing that Christmas sells in off months. Christmas collectors now search eBay all year, hoping to pick up bargains.

I put the bells on eBay in twelve different auctions, each starting at $9.99. The auctions ended on February 4th with no takers. I immediately relisted them to end one week later, on February 11th, but this time I started the auctions at $1.99 each. I was motivated to sell them and thought that starting the auctions really low might garner some interest.

On Wednesday, February 9th, I was looking at a calendar and realized that my kids were off that Friday for President's Day. I started thinking, "We haven't been to Mexico recently—I wonder how much airfare is these days?" I got on Orbitz.com and found a great price of $250 round-trip from LAX to Puerto Vallarta. I also found a great five-star hotel for $250 a night. The plane would leave on Thursday at 2 PM—which gave us less than 24 hours to get ready. I called my mom and said, "Are you in?" Definitely!

The last people to convince

were my kids, Houston and Indy. Going on the trip would mean missing Thursday and Monday from school. Monday was Valentine's Day, and it is always one of their favorite holidays.

It was a tough sell, but they finally agreed! I told them to get packed, and within one hour we were all ready to go.

We stayed at a beautiful hotel. Unfortunately, it wasn't on the beach, but the hotel had golf carts for shuttling guests to an amazing private beach club. No one told us until we arrived at the hotel, however, that the private beach was for adults only. I was livid. We ended up hanging out at our pool and the famous Nikki Beach Club instead. We had a blast on our trip, but I was still very mad about the beach club being adults-only. So when I returned home I filed a complaint with Orbitz, stating that if they had included that information on their web site, I would not have booked that hotel. I couldn't believe it, but they agreed with me. They refunded the entire $1,000 of the hotel price.

After spending that first vacation day by the pool, I decided to check on my auctions and headed into the business center. I couldn't believe that these items had sold for $186.

The lady who purchased them told me that she collects anything with a "Twelve Days of Christmas" theme and keeps her collections up on display all year. She was thrilled to get these. I was thrilled to get such a good price for these bells—especially when we were floating around a pool on vacation!

#84 Freckled Felines Plate

$2.00 Paid

From: Garage sale

Freckled Felines Franklin Mint Laurel Burch Cat Plate

Description:

Freckled Felines Franklin Mint Laurel Burch Cat Plate is from 1996. HA 3973. Darling. 8 ⅛" and in great condition. Could use a slight cleaning. No box.

Winning Bid:

$76.00

Ended: 2/15/05
History: 12 bids
Starting Bid: $9.99
Winner: Texas

Viewed

000177 X

Freckled Felines Plate #84

The Story

I saw this $2 plate at a garage sale in a neighborhood called "the state streets." We don't usually find much in this area, which has a street named for each and every one of the 50 states. It is laid out incredibly poorly, and the streets wind around and dead-end in strange places. It makes absolutely no sense. My mom and I always joke that whoever planned the layout must have been drunk.

During the 1970's, collector's plates commanded wildly inflated prices. The 1971 Goebel Hummel plate, for example, used to bring in over $1,000. Now it is hardly worth $100. You will see a lot of collector's plates priced too high at garage sales. Most won't sell for $9.99 (my usual auction starting price), but many sellers who bought their plates during the collector's plate "bubble" think their plates are still worth a fortune. And I have found from years and years of experience that if someone thinks their item is really, really good, it usually isn't.

Of course, some collector's plates have retained their value. Older years of Bing & Grondahl and Royal Copenhagen can still bring in the money. You must know what you are doing when dealing with collector's plates.

This plate was priced fairly and I recognized the name Laurel Burch. It didn't come with the original box or paperwork—most importantly, the COA (certificate of authenticity). These items can be very critical to a serious collector. Even without the box, I knew that

Burch was a pretty collectible artist so I decided to buy it.

I will tell you that I hemmed and hawed and would have bought it a lot quicker if it had been $1. The cats on the plate reminded me of my fat high school cat, Brubaker. For some reason, our family only ever had orange tabby cats. Could it be because four out of five of us have red hair? I think so! We started with Tigger, then Barney (he ran away quickly), and finally Brubaker. He was an awesome cat!

Laurel Burch began creating jewelry in the 1960's that she sold on the streets of San Francisco. Even though Laurel has never taken an art course, she has an unmistakable style that features a lot of mythical animals. Her designs can be found on jewelry, note cards, clothing, tote bags, mugs, and silk scarves, not to mention collector's plates. As a side note, almost any notable artist who was designing prior to the 1970's has their artwork on a collector's plate. Norman Rockwell, Thomas Kinkade, and Jody Bergsma are just a few others.

This auction ended the day we returned from Mexico and I was excited to find that my $2 investment had sold for $76. What a great homecoming!

#85 Knitting Mouse Ornament

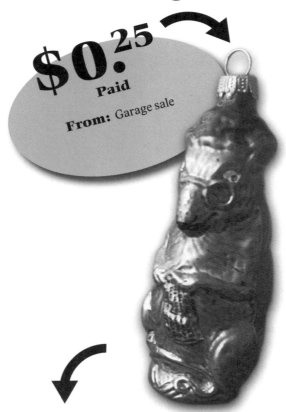

$0.²⁵

Paid

From: Garage sale

German Blown Glass Mice Mouse Ornament Knitting Germany

Description:

German blown glass knitting mouse Christmas ornament. This is a 4" super-cute ornament. Knitting is so "in" right now and here is a little grey mouse knitting in a red Christmas Santa hat. In excellent condition. Marked "Made in Germany" on the top of the ornament hook.

Winning Bid:

$25.⁵⁶

Ended: 2/15/05
History: 4 bids
Starting Bid: $9.99
Winner: Pennsylvania

Viewed
000062 X

Knitting Mouse Ornament #85

The Story

At the same garage sale in the state streets where I bought the Laurel Burch plate, I found this Christmas ornament. Glass Christmas ornaments are often marked with country of origin on the brass ornament crown. If it says Hong Kong, Taiwan, China or Korea, I usually pass. If it is marked Germany, I will buy it for a reasonable price.

This little knitting mouse was only 25 cents and it was marked "Made in Germany." Of course I bought it. I knew that there are a ton of mouse collectors and that knitting is really in vogue these days.

Knitting has been around, primarily as an occupation for women, since almost the third century; it may have originated in Persia. Initially, knitting was mainly used to make socks. Later, its uses diversified, and knitters began making sweaters, cardigans, and blankets. In recent years, knitting has shed its former dowdy image and gained a reputation as a fun and stylish activity; Hollywood trendsetters are among those who have taken it up.

Christmas in Germany has been synonymous with blown glass ornaments since the 1500's. Germany has long been the major world source for these ornaments, which were first made by artisans after the invention of the blowpipe. In Germany, ornament blowing began as a cottage industry in the town of Lauscha, and then spread through most of the countryside.

Now, we know why the knitting aspect of this item is important and why a German blown glass ornament is special—but what about the fact that the ornament portrayed a mouse? It turns out there are many, many mouse collectors. The mouse is physically small and timid, unassuming and plain—but also quite cute!

So this item carried a triple wallop—it was collectible for three different reasons. Check out #6 in my first *100 Best* book for another knitting mouse that sold for over $200! I may be on to something here! If you can find items that are collectible for more than two different reasons, you will have a winner. I sure did when 25 cents turned into over $25.

Christmas was always special in my family, and we would travel hours, if not days, to spend it with our grandmother. She always had a variety of tricks up her sleeve that she would pull out on Christmas day. One trick was to wrap a tiny box inside a slightly bigger box and then inside a huge box. Another one of her favorites was the old marble trick.

I just found her original marble trick box. It had a poinsettia decoration on the outside, and when you shook it, four marbles would roll around to drive you crazy as you tried to figure out what it was. Once you opened it, you would find a silly note from her, and then everyone would laugh and laugh. Oftentimes, my grandmother's trick gifts were even more fun than ones that actually cost money!

#86   1971 Towle Medallion

$2.00 Paid

From: Garage sale

First in a Series of Christmas Medallions by Towle Silversmiths

1971 FE Mint in Box Towle Sterling Xmas Medallion RARE

Description:
This Towle Sterling Christmas Medallion is very rare. Hard to find. It comes in the original box with great felt pouch and paperwork. 2 ½". In excellent condition. There is a partridge in a pear tree on one side and a dove on the other. Marked "Sterling Towle."

Winning Bid:

$146.⁹⁴

Ended: 2/25/05
History: 8 bids
Starting Bid: $9.99
Winner: Virginia

Viewed

000077 X

1971 Towle Medallion #86

The Story

I was out on a Saturday morning garage saling, and I was exhausted. I had stayed up until 2 AM talking on the phone (not thinking about my 6 AM wake-up call). Do you remember the days when you could get by on four hours of sleep? I was out of practice, and I was paying for it.

I was having a hard time concentrating on the items at one garage sale, but I did spot a red thin box with the name "Towle" and the word "sterling" on it. I recognized it immediately as a Christmas ornament. I knew that some Towle ornaments (even the silver plated ones) could sell for hundreds of dollars. This one was only $2. Boy, was I glad that I had woken up early and decided to go saling—even in my exhausted state.

The Towle silversmith name goes back to 1690! Towle is an American company founded by William Moulton II in Newbury, Massachusetts. Six consecutive generations of Moulton silversmiths followed using the Towle name. Wow! This company was older than America itself.

When everyone was getting into the collectibles business in the 1970's, Towle began designing sterling Christmas ornaments. The 1971 ornament that I bought featured a partridge in a pear tree; it was the first in the series that portrayed the twelve days of Christmas. A first edition (FE) of any series is usually a good seller.

During the thirteen years I lived in LA, I did not miss one Christmas with my grandma. It was one of her favorite days of the year (along with her birthday). No matter what it took, I would fly home for the holidays. When I was in retail, sometimes that would mean flying at very odd times, but I knew it was important to my grandmother.

She would spend weeks preparing our gifts. In later years, she used her dining room table as her desk. It had a plastic tablecloth and underneath it, she hid note cards labeled with each of our names. On each card, she would keep track of the gifts she had for that person. She wanted to make sure she was fair. She was just like Santa Claus, checking and re-checking her lists. Every year, she would pick one gift to give to each one of us. One year it was a waffle maker, another year an electric fry pan. But mostly, we received antiques and collectibles. Of course!

I collected teddy bears, and one Christmas she hand-sewed a hot pink plush jointed teddy bear for me. What a grandma! Another Christmas she gave me a bear named "Boo" who could put his hands over his eyes to play peek-a-boo. I took that bear to college with me, and I still have him. One year, I found a "Boo" bear to give back to her. She was so thrilled. And I was thrilled when this $2 item sold for almost $150! Boo hoo, all the way to the bank.

#87 3 Skeleton Keys

$0.00 Paid
From: Inheritance

2 50 each

3 Neat Antique Cast Iron Skeleton Key Keys 1880's NICE

Description:
3 Neat Antique Cast Iron Skeleton Key Keys from about 1880's to 1900's. Some rust. 4 ¼" to 4 ⅝".

Winning Bid:

$20.⁹⁵
Ended: 2/28/05
History: 8 bids
Starting Bid: $9.99
Winner: Massachusetts

Viewed

000091 X

The Story

These keys were in one of my inherited boxes. They were so cute and still packaged the way my grandmother used to sell them. She had tons of old keys for sale in the primitive section of the shop. She would put all the similar keys on a round metal wire and put just one price tag on them. The tag would indicate the price for EACH item. It was a huge timesaver. These keys were tagged at $2.50 each—still in her handwriting.

I immediately knew to call them skeleton keys. Wow! Where did I remember that from? A skeleton key (or passkey) is a key with a very simple design that usually has a cylindrical shaft and a single flat, rectangular tooth. It is used for the easiest type of lock, which only provides very minimal security because items other than the actual key can fit into the lock and open it. This type of key fell out of favor when more complicated locks became easier to manufacture (about 1920).

When I was in first grade at Monmouth Elementary School, they tried an experimental program to teach children to read and write. What a mistake! It was called ITA (Initial Teaching Alphabet) and it ruined my spelling skills for life. We were taught to spell using 44 sound symbols instead of the real 26-letter alphabet. There were strange symbols like "ae," "ee," "ie," "ou," and so on.

I used to write letters to my grandma and grandpa using this alphabet;

they would need a key just to figure out what I was trying to say. It was atrocious. I was a terrible speller for many years and I blame ITA. If you can believe it, the card here says "Happy Birthday Grandma, Love Lynn Lee Sharon Wayne Kristin."

I realize that the ITA people believed that their system made the complex subject of spelling simpler. In the same way, skeleton keys were made to be quite simple. Both should now be obsolete. Most skeleton keys are. However, I see that ITA is still in business.

Let's get back to the other simple keys. I guessed that they were 1880's to 1900's and I also noted in the description that they were rusty. I was very happy when $7.50 worth of keys

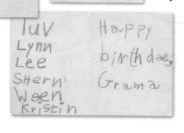

(at retail) sold for $20.95! I am even happier that over the years, I have learned to spell quite well. Practice makes perfect. I was just complaining to my mom and dad about ITA and saying what a terrible speller it made me. My kids jumped into the conversation and said, "Mommy, you are an awesome speller—you know how to spell everything." That made me feel great!

#88 Royal Bayreuth Moose

$1.⁰⁰ Paid

From: Garage sale

Royal Bayreuth Bavaria Pitcher Moose Elk Figural OLD!

Description:

Royal Bayreuth Bavarian Pitcher is figural with a moose or elk. This antique piece is missing 7 horns and is being sold as is. There is a small chip at the lower lip also. 8 ¾" by 7". An elk, deer or moose. Still a neat antique piece. Hopefully someone can repair him. 1900's to 1920's.

Winning Bid:

$39.⁰⁰

Ended: 3/7/05
History: 10 bids
Starting Bid: $9.99
Winner: Arkansas

Viewed
 **X**

Royal Bayreuth Moose #88

The Story

I found this Royal Bayreuth Moose at a garage sale for $1. We had carried a lot of Royal Bayreuth pieces in the antiques store over the years. They made tomato and lobster pieces that I remembered from my childhood. I knew that figural pieces (those shaped like animals, vegetables, fruits, flowers, or people) could sell for quite a lot of money. So, even though this was very "as is," with chips and missing horns, I bought it anyway.

Royal Bayreuth was founded in Tettau, Germany in 1794. It is the oldest china producer under private ownership and is still considered one of Germany's finest producers of quality porcelain. Their figural items were produced from about 1880 to the beginning of World War I (1917). Many of their pieces were not marked, or marked only with "Deponiert" or "Registered."

In 1974, Royal Bayreuth came out with a Sunbonnet Babies plate series which showed babies doing different activities for each day of the week—Monday was washing, Tuesday ironing, Wednesday mending, Thursday scrubbing, Friday sweeping, Saturday baking and Sunday was fishing. Man, am I glad that I am NOT a Sunbonnet Baby and that I rarely do any of these things!

My grandmother carried those plates in her store and did quite well with

them. Back in the day, we could get close to $100 per plate. Now, I see the entire series selling on eBay for just over $200—which is not a bad price in today's very different plate market.

I was pleasantly surprised when the moose ended up selling for $39. The man who bought him had a sense of humor, and emailed me immediately to find out about how quickly he could receive his "crippled" moose. He was planning to make him "as good as new."

My grandmother was in a wheelchair for the last fifteen years of her life. She got breast cancer in 1980 and survived that. In 1985, they found that the breast cancer had spread to her lungs, and that fight is the one that put her in a wheelchair. She survived that. In 1990, she found that the breast cancer had spread to her hip bones, and amazingly enough, she survived that also. She was an incredible fighter and often said, "I'm a survivor." Being in a wheelchair did not keep her from living her life to the fullest or helping me with my kids. Her lap was one of their favorite places to be.

After each battle, she would also emerge "as good as new." I know that she would have related to this moose.

#89 Supertramp Sheet Music

$0.³⁰ Paid

From: Garage sale

Supertramp Sheet Music Logical Song Breakfast America

Description:
Supertramp sheet music is for "The Logical Song" (Almo Music, 1979) by Roger Hodgson & Rick Davies. The cover is "Breakfast in America" with the waitress. From 1979; in good to very good condition with some wear. We have a lot of sheet music up for sale this week. Please check out our other auctions. Most of the sheet music is from the 1920's to 1930's.

Winning Bid:

$23.⁰⁶

Ended: 3/10/05
History: 3 bids
Starting Bid: $9.99
Winner: California

Viewed

 X

Supertramp Sheet Music   #89

The Story

This item sure reminded me of my teen years. I found it mixed in with a suitcase full of sheet music from the 1920's to 1930's I bought at a garage sale for $30. There were about 100 pieces, meaning this sheet had only cost me 30 cents. I like selling paper goods because they are relatively easy to store, and they're very easy to ship. Maureen likes them also!

This piece of sheet music was the only modern one in the entire bunch, and it's the one that sold for the most money. Sheet music is just the printed or written form of a musical composition. Generally, each piece of sheet music records just a single song or piece. Sheet music is most often produced for voice, piano, and guitar compositions (or a combination of the three). Many sheet music collectors actually use the music, but collectors also frame it to use as decoration in their homes or offices. Some of the artwork on the covers is fantastic.

I was forced as a child to play the piano; during middle school, I played the clarinet. Check out my report card from 7th grade band. I was actually "above average minus" in something and way too close to being average. Yikes! Believe me, I am not musically inclined. Music is my absolute worst subject—I have no inherent talent. I took piano for about four years, and what I remember most about those lessons is that many times my mom or dad would forget to pick me up. Some-

times, I would spend hours waiting in the rain. There were no cell phones then. Maybe this is one reason that I am not a big fan of music. Today, however, I am grateful that I can read music. I think this is a good skill to have.

Supertramp was a band put together in England in 1969. Backed by a Dutch millionaire, it began with just two members, Rick Davies and Roger Hodgson. Many members came and went over the years. The band's name comes from a 1908 novel by W.H. Davies called *The Autobiography of a Super-Tramp*. The book explored the life of an intelligent man who decided to live a relatively simple life during the time of railway building in America.

Supertramp (the band) didn't attain commercial success for quite a few years. Their best-selling album "Breakfast in America" came out in 1979 and hit number one in the United States. This album has sold over eighteen million copies.

Since this sheet music was for one of Supertramp's most popular songs from their most popular album, it is no wonder that it sold for over $20. I also think that the campy photography on the cover helped to drive up the price. This band was definitely above average plus—if not high (outstanding)—in the 1970's!

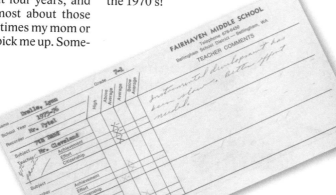

#90 Last Supper Plates

$20.00 Paid

From: Boutique area at charity sale

Veneto Flair Scene 5 V The Last Supper Plate 1976 Jesus

Description:
Veneto Flair Scene 5 is from "The Last Supper" series—DaVinci's Last Supper as interpreted by V. Tiziano. The Veneto Flair Collector's plates are some of the most beautiful in the world. Made by hand on a potter's wheel in Italy. These plates were very, very expensive when first issued and not very many of them were made. In perfect condition. 8 ¾" and comes with the certificate of authenticity and the velvet bag. No box. We have all 5 scenes in this hard-to-find series up for sale this week. They are being sold separately. The plates all have the same serial number.

Winning Bid: **$519.50/5**

Ended: 3/13/05
History: 82 bids/5
Starting Bid: $9.99 each
Winner: Florida

Viewed
 X

Last Supper Plates #90

The Story

I found this set of plates at one of the big charity church sales here in our valley. After I had scoured the entire gym full of regular items, I headed over to the boutique area. There on the floor under a table was a box full of Veneto Flair collector's plates.

I know my Veneto Flair. My grandmother was a good friend of Lee Benson, the company's founder. He would often call her when new issues were coming out because he could always count on her for a big order. I just came across one of my grandma's scrap papers with Lee's phone number and an order for two dozen of the stag plate—an order worth $500 wholesale. She was one of Veneto Flair's top-ten dealers and was always offered exclusives before the rest of the country. I told you before, she did really, really well in the collector's plate business.

Veneto Flair was different from the other plate companies at that time. All their items were hand-turned on ancient pottery wheels using native terra cotta clay dug from the hills in Deruta, Italy. Then the intricate and beautiful designs were etched on the plates entirely by hand. The deep rich colors were also hand painted and each piece was heavily accented with pure gold. The final touch was to hand-write all the information about each individual plate on its back side. These plates were truly works of art.

The original retail prices for these plates were quite high in the 1970's, ranging from $45 to $60. What was great about Veneto Flair was that Benson didn't allow tens of thousands of pieces to be made. Most plates were made in runs of only 1,000 to 2,000 pieces. That is why some of these plates are still quite valuable today.

My grandmother carried almost every single plate that they made. Of the "Last Supper" series, however, we had only had three of the five plates. I was thrilled to find the complete set of five, all of which had the same serial number (meaning that they were originally sold together). To get the bidding going, I decided to sell them in individual auctions. I knew that someone would desperately want to acquire all five. I was right! I love it when that happens.

The plate that sold for the most was number five, which showed Jesus and was intended to be displayed in the center of the other four. It sold for $197.50. I received the same amount—over $500—for my five plates that my grandmother spent for 24 plates in the 1970's!

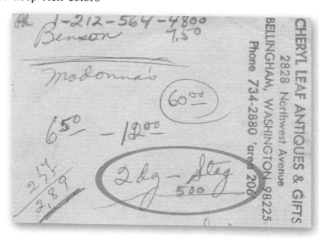

#91 3 Horse Brasses

$1.00 Paid
From: Garage sale

Old Brass Horse Harness Decoration Shakespeare's House

Description:
Old horse harness decoration is brass and shows Shakespeare's house at Stratford on Avon. Probably English, but not marked. It is vintage. 3 ⅛" by 2 ¾". It needs cleaning and has some tarnish. In overall good to very good condition. Darling. We have two other ones also up for sale in separate auctions.

Winning Bid:

$49.⁴⁹/3

Ended: 3/16/05
History: 19 bids/3
Starting Bid: $4.99 each
Winners: OR, GA

Viewed
000136 X

The Story

So many little girls are animal crazy, and horses seem to be the animal they love most. I was never horse crazy as a girl. My sister was, and I think that Indiana is going to be also. My sister rode horses for much of her childhood. She currently has one dog, six cats and two guinea pigs—and she is an adult. My daughter is begging me for a dog and I am saying, "NO!"— We can hardly take care of our ancient cat. Indiana is definitely following in her Auntie Kiki's footsteps.

These three horse brasses were taped together with masking tape and marked $1 when I saw them. I could tell that they were brass and that they were most likely horse harness decorations. Animal collectors and animal lovers are a great bunch of buyers. They will bid an awful lot of money when they decide that they want something.

I had learned what horse harness decorations were many years before when I came across a shoebox full of them in the snake pit. I had asked my grandmother, "Are these belt buckles?" She had laughed and said, "No, they are for decorating a horse's tack and harness." "You have got to be kidding. What will they think of next?" I thought. But these were antique, so it should have been, "What were they thinking?"

People first began to decorate their horses' harnesses in the 1750's. Originally, they did it to bring good luck or to ward off the effects of the "evil eye." As cultures became less superstitious, tack and harness decorations were used primarily to show off the quality of one's horse and the wealth of the owner. Interesting! Brass ornamentation caught on in England around 1800. These decorations were most popular from 1850 to 1910, and were mass-produced by either stamping or casting.

I thought that mine were most likely English because one showed Shakespeare's house, and the lion was actually stamped "England." I couldn't put my finger on an actual date for these, so I just called them "old," and that seemed to do the trick.

None of them sold the first time at auction for $9.99, so I relisted them all at a starting bid of $4.99 each. They all found buyers the second time around. The Shakespeare horse brass sold for the most, $24.50. The crossed keys went for $20, and the lion for $4.99. Grand total: almost $50! Now, if I can just talk Indiana into a virtual dog, life will be perfect.

#92 Slingshot

$0.⁰⁰
Paid
From: Inheritance

Rustic Folk Art Carved Wooden Slingshot Antique CUTE

Description:
Rustic carved sling shot is 11" by 4 ½" by 1". It is in very good condition. Missing the leather or rubber sling portion. I would guess 1900's to 1940's. Folk art. Americana.

Winning Bid:

$9.⁹⁹
Ended: 3/17/05
History: 1 bid
Starting Bid: $9.99 store price
Winner: Georgia

Viewed
 **X**

Slingshot #92

The Story

I found this slingshot in a box that I got from the shop. It was really rustic and handmade—most likely early American folk art. "Folk art" is a broad (and very wonderful) term to describe a range of artistic expression. It can be used to describe items from a particular country or region as well as from individual artists. Most folk artists have no formal training; they are just trying to record the ordinary activities of life. Most folk art pieces are both functional and artistic. There is a huge following for folk art items on eBay.

Many children's toys from my mother's generation would be considered folk art. She was born in the 1930's, and most of the things she played with were handmade, artistic and functional. Relatively few were mass-produced. I loved the teddy bear she had as a baby and it is now in my office. This old photo of her with "Mr. Bear" is one of my favorites; I love her contemplative look. Unfortunately, a dog got to "Mr. Bear" and ripped him apart shortly after this photo was taken, but we still have this wonderful image to remember him.

I had tried selling the slingshot at auction, but there were no takers. I had never thought of using eBay stores to sell one-of-a-kind, unique items. But when Mo started working for me in October, I decided to start trying more items in my eBay store.

For Pete's sake, it was only three cents a month for ANY starting price point and a gallery picture. I figured it would only cost me 36 cents per year for any item. It was worth a shot to try some of these more unique pieces in the store.

Immediately, we started to see great results. Dinnerware and other items that we thought would never sell were suddenly bringing in full price. In no time at all, we were selling $1,000 to $2,000 a month from our eBay store, and it wasn't taking any extra work (other than the usual shipping). All the work had already been done when we had listed it originally. There was no downside to using the eBay store.

Mo had listed this slingshot in the store in October of 2004, and it only took five months to sell! Mo's husband thought it was so interesting that he announced he was going into the business of making hand-carved slingshots. I hated to tell him that I didn't think the market was that strong—but you just never know.

What is a slingshot anyway? A slingshot is a small-hand powered weapon. It typically has some type of pocket at the end of the rubber to hold the ammunition. My slingshot did not have the rubber or a pocket. A slingshot can be powerful enough to hunt small game. Who knew?

#93 Tiki Seahorse

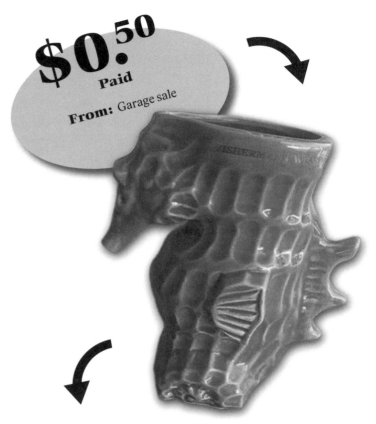

$0.⁵⁰ Paid

From: Garage sale

Tiki Sea Horse Hawaii Tumbler Fisherman's Wharf Honolulu

Description:
Tiki sea horse Hawaiian drink tumbler is a great turquoise blue color. Says "Fisherman's Wharf," "Kewalo Basin," and "Honolulu, Hawaii" on it. Louie B Ceramics. In excellent condition. Slight wear and needs cleaning. Really neat! Vintage.

Winning Bid: $42.⁹⁹

Ended: 3/23/05
History: 10 bids
Starting Bid: $9.99
Winner: Michigan

Viewed

000075 X

The Story

It was tennis time out here in the desert. Every March, the Pacific Life Open brings great players to Indian Wells. During those two weeks, I love to see as much tennis as possible. My absolute favorite player is Andre Agassi, because he is from my generation (well—more or less). I have been following his career since I was in college. He seems like such a nice person, and yet he's an extremely fierce competitor.

Melanie was in town for business, happy to escape the freezing weather in Philadelphia. We got tickets for the Saturday session and were lucky enough to see Agassi play. It was a blast. Earlier that morning, I had dragged her along to...you know...garage sales!

She is such a trooper, and up for anything. It is always fun when she tags along with my mom and me. She keeps us laughing. At one garage sale, I spotted this piece for only 50 cents. I know that Hawaiian items sell very well, and this was a totally cute tumbler. I bought it, and we headed home. I was forced to sit on the floor of the minivan because I had bought

Fisherman's Wharf

Honolulu, Hawaii

a huge shelf that morning and it took up the entire back space. Melanie just rolls her eyes when I do stuff like this. She has known me for far too long!

I called it a "tiki sea horse" even though it wasn't a true "tiki." In Polynesian culture, "tiki" is both the name of the first man as well as a sculptural image animated by a spirit. In the South Pacific during the 1930's and 1940's, many restaurants with a tropical Polynesian theme opened. Polynesian décor featured torches, rattan furniture, leis, bright fabrics—and tikis.

About this time, many soldiers were returning home from World War II and brought stories and souvenirs from the South Pacific along with them. America fell in love with the exotic designs, and what is called a "tiki culture" began. When Hawaii became our 50th state in 1959, this frenzy skyrocketed. Anything tiki-inspired took center stage, and all those old war souvenirs became hot items! Tiki items are still very collectible today.

The restaurant that my pseudo-tiki came from, The Fisherman's Wharf in Honolulu, also has an interesting history. The restaurant's architecture fits the tropical "tiki culture" theme perfectly. I phoned the restaurant, and found that it is still in business. It was opened in 1952, and these tumblers were given away with drinks from the 1990's to about 2001. The woman I spoke to said that they had stopped giving the mugs away because the manufacturer, Louie B, had gone out of business. I said, "That's funny, because I found their web site and they still make and sell them for only $4 each."

Hmmmm, maybe I should be buying these wholesale and selling them on eBay. The one I sold with the name of the restaurant brought in $42.99! I told you: Hawaiiana and tikis are very collectible.

#94   3 Tiffany & Co. Items

$1.50 Paid

From: Garage sale

Signed Tiffany & Co Crystal Heart Hearts Bowl LOVELY

Description:
This signed Tiffany & Co. crystal heart bowl is lovely. It is in excellent condition. It has 16 embossed or raised glass hearts. 5" by 3". No chips, no cracks, no crazing.

Winning Bid:

$69.00/3

Ended: 3/23/05
History: 16 bids/3
Starting Bid: $9.99 each
Winner: CA, AZ and IN

Viewed
000202 X

The Story

The week that these Tiffany items were selling on eBay was the same week that I was being heavily quoted in an article for *The National Enquirer.* How cool is that? I love reading the tabloids. I admit it. Oddly enough, my grandmother was the original tabloid reader in our family. She had a few subscriptions—*The Star* and *The National Enquirer* were her favorites. When I was home visiting from LA, I would often sit on the couch in her living room and read them.

So it was super neat to have my comments take up half a page in the *NE.* My grandmother would have thought it was so cool! How did this come about? Well, the road to *The Enquirer* was quite long. I had hired a really great publicist, Meg McAllister, in July of 2004. She and her company got me quite a lot of great print, and this was one of the articles. It was called "11 Things You Should Never Buy Used." I was quoted talking about health hazards, warranty issues and other important concerns relating to certain types of consumer goods.

Things that you *should* buy used are all the antiques and collectibles that are found on eBay. It is also a great place to find brand new gift items that the original recipients of the gifts didn't want. I was lucky enough to stumble across a gift basket full of brand new Tiffany items at a garage sale. It was only $1.50 for three items: a tablecloth, a crystal heart bowl, and an oversized cup and saucer.

I knew that two of the pieces were authentic Tiffany because the bowl still had the Tiffany sticker and the tablecloth was also marked "Tiffany & Co." I wasn't sure about the oversized cup and saucer because it had no maker's marks, so I listed it with that information in the description.

I love Tiffany items. Who doesn't? Tiffany & Co. has been around for a long time; it came out with the first issue of its now very famous catalog in 1845. It is most well known for its blue boxes with white bows, the Tiffany-style engagement ring (which debuted in 1886), and the 1950 Truman Capote novel *Breakfast at Tiffany's.* The movie based on the book (which starred Audrey Hepburn) wasn't made until 1961. Whichever way you look at it, Tiffany has become a brand name synonymous with classic quality.

I couldn't believe that these three Tiffany pieces, purchased for just 50 cents each, ended up selling for $69! And I was in *The National Enquirer.* Classy and trashy. What a combination!

#95 Mint Julep Cups

$5.⁰⁰ **Paid**

From: Church rummage sale

Horse Stoneware Kentucky Derby 2 Mint Julep Cups Recipe

Description:
These 2 mint julep cups or mugs are so neat. Louisville stoneware for the Kentucky Derby. These two match; they have mint plants & leaves on the front and the recipe for mint juleps on the back. I have shown the front of one and the back of one. Green edge. In excellent condition. 4 ⅛".

Winning Bid:

$90.⁰⁰/3

Ended: 3/31/05
History: 30 bids/3
Starting Bid: $9.99 each
Winner: Georgia

Viewed

000078 X

Mint Julep Cups   #95

The Story

The Kentucky Derby—what an all-American event. It garners the attention of the nation, if not the world, and only takes two minutes—although some claim that they are the most exciting two minutes in sports. It has always amazed me that this race is responsible for so many trips, parties, and hat sales.

It was a Saturday in March (the Derby is always held on the first Saturday of May), and I had finally talked my assistant into attending some sales with me. Maureen ("Mo") had been doing an awesome job, but I felt that she should be exposed to the process of finding merchandise as well as selling and packaging it. I wanted to teach her more about eBay, so someday she could do it on her own. I know—not smart as far as my own business goes. But I want to encourage her.

The first sale was at the Presbyterian church. It started at 8 AM. Mo hates getting up early almost as much (if not more than) I do, so my mom and I were already waiting in line when she showed up at 7:50 AM. It was just in the nick of time; the sellers had decided to let us all in early. Away we went!

Mo found several things for me that day as she learned. One was a pitcher for 10 cents (it is the next story). The first sale was disappointing, however, so we headed clear across town to the charity sale at the Lutheran church.

That sale was so much fun. They had been open for a while and hadn't moved a lot of merchandise. So, believe you me—they were thrilled to see some dealers who were actually spending money. Us! The people running the Lutheran charity sale were incredibly nice and accommodating. We filled up about four boxes and were on our way out when someone told us that there was a boutique area inside. Oh, no! Not another boutique area!

We decided to give it a shot. Things looked interesting, but overpriced (as usual). Mo found three mint julep mugs priced at $5 and asked, "What do you think?" I said, "I don't know." Then Mo told me that when her son Kelly was little he was obsessed with horses. Almost all of his toddler photos were taken with a horse! She knew that Derby items were really in demand. I still didn't think that they would sell, but she seemed to have some insider information. So I told her, "Let's try them." Remember, this was supposed to be a learning experience for Mo, and the best way to learn is by trial and error.

Well, turns out that Mo knows more than I do. Those three mint julep mugs sold for $90. Amazing! Mo will be leaving me any day now to start her own eBay business. Just kidding (I hope!)

#96 Advertising Pitcher

$0.10
Paid

From: Church rummage sale

Advertising OLD Creamware Pitcher Lumber Coal Feed IN

Description:
Old advertising creamware pitcher says, "Compliments of Melvin Myers & Sons Dealers Lumber Coal Feed Miami, Indiana." This is such a neat piece of early advertising memorabilia. It has 2 chips. One is on the spout, about ⅜" by ¼", and one is on the edge, ½" by ⅜". I would guess early turn of the century 1900's.

Winning Bid:

$45.05
Ended: 4/05/05
History: 5 bids
Starting Bid: $9.99
Winner: Indiana

Viewed
 **X**

Advertising Pitcher #96

The Story

I was born in Indiana in the city of Bloomington, while my dad was getting his doctorate and my mom her masters from Indiana University. We left Indiana when I was only a year old. I don't remember anything about living there, but I have been back a few times and it is a beautiful state.

I loved the name Indiana and wanted to use it for one of my children. I thought it would work for either a boy or a girl. I also wanted to honor my grandmother in the naming of one of my children, but neither "Cheryl" nor "Eldonna" (my grandma's middle name) seemed to be good choices. So we looked at her other family members. Her brother Houston was named for our distant relative Sam Houston, of "Battle of the Alamo" fame. Houston was a strong family name, and I thought it was the perfect choice when my firstborn was a son.

When my next baby was a girl, Indiana just seemed to be the perfect name and it fit well with Houston. She is very independent, and we call her Indy for short.

So it was funny when Mo picked up this pitcher from Miami, Indiana, at the church sale. It was priced at only 10 cents because it was chipped. She thought we should try it, and once again, I didn't think it was going to sell because of the damage. But I wanted Mo to learn about the importance of condition firsthand, so I bought it.

I listed it on eBay with "advertising" and "creamware" featured in the title. I left out the actual name of the company and put the types of items it sold—lumber, coal and feed—into the heading instead. I also managed to include IN (for Indiana) in the title—sometimes I call my daughter In for short!

Advertising collectibles are very desirable, and lumber and coal items are rare. The combination of lumber, coal and feed made it even more unique. Miami, Indiana is a very small town; according to the 2000 census, only 1,305 people live there.

Creamware is a creamy white earthenware pottery made in the Staffordshire region of England; it was eventually perfected by Wedgwood. It is also known as "queensware" or "Prattware" and its heyday was between 1750 and 1820. Cream-colored pottery can still be called creamware, and it is very collectible.

I couldn't believe it when this "as is" piece sold for $45.05. There went my "only good condition sells" lesson for Mo. Just think what it would have been worth if it had been perfect—it might have been priceless. Just like my kids!

#97 Hoya Crystal Horse

$5.⁰⁰ Paid

From: Estate sale

Hoya Crystal Stylized Eames Era Figure Japan WOW!

Description:
Hoya crystal horse is very stylized and Eames-era in design. This is an amazing crystal figurine or sculpture. It is 5" by 4 ¼" by 1 ¾". It is very heavy and signed "Hoya Japan Crystal." Signed in etching and with a sticker. In excellent condition.

Winning Bid:

$76.⁰⁰

Ended: 4/13/05
History: 13 bids
Starting Bid: $9.99
Winner: New York

Viewed

000134 X

The Story

As this second *100 Best* book comes to an end, I am feeling nostalgic and a little sad. I always have so much fun dragging out the boxes and boxes (you know my grandmother) of photos, letters and snippets of papers that she saved over the years. I can get lost for hours looking at everything and deciding which things work best with each story. It is not as sad as it was three years ago when I wrote the first *100 Best*. It is getting easier to see these things and not cry. I still miss my grandmother dearly, but it has gotten better.

In one of the boxes I found a postcard that she hadn't mailed (probably because it had gotten lost!). It had a two-cent stamp on it, meaning it was written between 1952 and 1958. It was addressed to the Marble Collegiate Church in New York, NY. That is the church that Norman Vincent Peale pastored. About two years ago, my friend Juliette told me that I should read his book *The Power of Positive Thinking*. I did, and then proceeded to read many of his other writings. They are all very positive and wonderful. I had even sent away for his "Thought Conditioners," which is forty powerful spiritual phrases he wrote in 1951 that can change the quality of your life!

I have always had a very positive outlook on life, but Peale's readings have helped to reinforce it. Sometimes it does get discouraging when we go out on a Saturday morning and don't find anything. I just keep thinking positively and know that the next weekend will be great. I found this horse during one of those "great weekends."

It was at an estate sale in Indian Wells. There aren't very many sales in Indian Wells because city law states that they must be held inside. We stumbled upon an amazing one and everything in the house was absolutely first rate in quality. The prices were fair and I loaded up. I found this crystal horse, signed "Hoya" and "Japan," for $5.

I couldn't find out anything much about Hoya, because the Hoya website was written entirely in Japanese! I did find that Hoya is known for its crystal-clear transparency and purity. I also found that there is a huge following on eBay for this type of crystal. This horse ended up selling for $76! Thinking positively absolutely works.

When I turned over the postcard that my grandmother had never mailed to the Marble Collegiate Church, I was surprised to see that she was writing to order Peale's "Thought Conditioners." If I know my grandmother, she lost this one in a pile of papers and ended up sending another. Who knew that back in the early 1950's, she was practicing Peale's positive thinking? It all makes sense to me now. My dad has often said to me "You are too positive." Can that even be possible? I am glad that my grandmother was around to instill such great beliefs in me.

#98 Capodimonte Figurine

$5.⁰⁰ Paid

From: Estate sale

Italy Capodimonte Harlequin Pantalone Pierrot ? Figurine

Description:

Italy Capodimonte Harlequin, Pantalone or Pierrot figurine. Some type of clown. Made in Italy with the "N" and crown—Capodimonte, I believe. Brick red, yellow, white, and black. He is holding a stick. I don't know which of the figures he is—Harlequin, Pantalone or Pierrot? 5" by 1 ¾" by 2". In excellent condition. 1920's to 1950's I would guess—vintage/antique. Very neat piece.

Winning Bid: **$135.¹³**

Ended: 4/14/05
History: 22 bids
Starting Bid: $9.99
Winner: Texas

Viewed

 X

Capodimonte Figurine   #98

The Story

I was still at that great estate sale in Indian Wells and I was still thinking positively. Funny how that works! I spotted this figurine hiding on a bookshelf and he was also priced at $5. That was cheap enough for a quality collectible from Italy. I thought that the signature looked like the Capodimonte crown. Even better.

Capodimonte (also known as Capo-di-monte) was founded near Naples, Italy in 1743. They started out making soft paste figurines and dinnerware. The factory closed in the 1760's, but reopened in 1771 in order to produce both soft and hard paste porcelains. Many of the Capodimonte pieces were adorned with applied florals. Their original mark was a crown over an "N" (for Naples). The original factory closed in 1821, and some of its molds were purchased by Docceia Porcelain in Florence.

The Capodimonte technique and signature have been copied so much over the years that "Capodimonte" has become something of a generic term. Most pieces you see today were made by other factories and are of more recent manufacture. Capodimonte pieces have been made in Hungary, Germany, France and Italy. I knew that this piece wasn't from the original factory, but I guessed that it dated from the 1920's to 1950's. At least it had been made in Italy and had the crown mark!

I bought a lot of things that day, but this piece sticks in my mind—probably because it sold for so much! But I also thought that it depicted a character from the famous Italian *Commedia dell'Arte* (Comedy of Art). I have a budding actress/singer as well as a budding sports star in my family. You have already heard about the baseball player, so I will tell you about the actress/singer. Indiana can put on a play at a moment's notice, and she does it quite often. She can use anything for a prop—from a hat to an umbrella—and before you know it, you are watching a musical. It makes life a lot of fun.

Commedia dell'Arte was a type of drama that originated in Italy and flourished for about 400 years, from the 14th to the 18th centuries, spreading to France and England. It was performed by a troupe of actors who traveled around putting on outdoor comedies based on conventional stock characters. The best known are Harlequin (an acrobat), Pulcinello (a mean hunchback), Pantalone (a shopkeeper), Columbine (Harlequin's girlfriend), and Pierrot (a dreamer and clown). The masked actors depicting these characters depended on improvisation rather than scripts to create their stories—just like Indiana!

I figured that this figurine was one of the stock characters, but couldn't figure out which one, so I put three different names in the title. There is a very large following for these characters, as I was to find out. This piece sold for $135.15 and I did a little dance with Indy!

#99   WWI Crest

$1.00 Paid

From: Garage sale

Unique Camp Jackson France 1917 Shield Crest WWI NEAT!

Description:

Unique Camp Jackson France crest is marked with "COL Camp Jackson 1917" and measures 10 ¾" by 11 ½". It also says, Valdahon France St. Michel Meuse Argonne 1918 Chattillon 1919 USA Demobilized. Help with this? We would really like to know what it is. It is strange with the metal piece that attaches on the top. It has come undone and needs to be fastened back with screws. It is also cracked. Red in color. I would guess World War I.

Winning Bid:

$107.27

Ended: 5/02/05
History: 14 bids
Starting Bid: $9.99
Winner: California

Viewed

 X

The Story

There is an antiques dealer here in Palm Desert who has really neat garage sales. He puts everything out on tables and believe me, there is tons of stuff. Then he invites buyers to make huge piles of what they want to buy. He then names a cheap price so the buyers will take it all away. He is obviously clearing out what is left of estates he has purchased—things that didn't sell in an antiques mall—and anything else that is gathering dust. It is a great way for him to get organized—and for me to get some bargains.

I found this piece on one of his tables on a Saturday morning. It looked really interesting, but it was broken. The metal top portion was falling off. Nevertheless, I bought it and it probably only cost me 50 cents to a dollar.

I put it on eBay with just the information that had been painted on it. I didn't do any research, but since the date was 1917 I could safely assume that it was a World War I piece. I couldn't believe it when it sold for $107.27! The gentleman that bought it filled me in on its history, and quite an interesting history it turned out to be. He also shared a photo of his collection with us. How neat!

On August 25, 1917, the 81st Infantry Division was organized at Camp (now Fort) Jackson in South Carolina. This draftee division was made up of unique individuals and they began a practice that was unheard of in those days. They started to wear a distinguishing shoulder patch—a black wildcat on an olive green circle. It caused a huge uproar and other units began to protest quite loudly.

Luckily, General John J. Pershing heard about it and approved their trademark! Moreover, he praised their *espirit de corps* and suggested that other Army divisions adopt patches. It turned out that the 81st Wildcats also distinguished themselves during the fighting in France and received the personal commendation of General Pershing. Their motto was "Obedience, Courage, Loyalty," and no wonder they were successful. What a great unit to have representing the United States of America, and a great thing to collect!

My grandmother always instilled in us a great pride in our country and reminded us how lucky we are to be Americans. She was extremely grateful to all the men and women who defended our country. Thanks to her, I realize what a privilege it is to live in the United States and I appreciate those who put their lives on the line in its service. Thank you to all our servicemen and women!

#100 Dualit Toaster

$2.⁰⁰ Paid

From: High school charity sale

Dualit Chrome Toaster Retro 4BR 84 London 4 Slice NEAT!

Description:
Dualit chrome toaster is really neat. This is a commercial toaster. Designed for commercial use, the toaster is hand assembled in England and built to last, with an insulated stainless steel body, variable controls and automatic turnoff. Rather than popping up, the toast stays warm inside for up to ten minutes. Slots accommodate thick bread as well as BAGELS! I think that these are the preferred toasters of Williams & Sonoma. Made in London. This toaster works great but has been used. Needs cleaning. These toasters retail for $319.00.

Winning Bid: **$192.⁵⁰**

Ended: 5/8/05
History: 14 bids
Starting Bid: $9.99
Winner: B.C., Canada

Viewed
 **X**

Dualit Toaster #100

The Story

It is so fitting that this is story #100, and I will tell you why. My dad was in town visiting and I was going out garage saling and needed some cash. Aren't parents just great to have around—for so many reasons? All he had was a $100 bill. I don't like to take big bills out with me, because often sellers can't make change. Also, I carry all my cash in my pockets, and a $100 bill would be a terrible thing to lose. But it was my only option at 6 AM, so I borrowed it from him.

One of our stops was an outdoor high school charity event. I found quite a few great items in the housewares area. This toaster had been there ever since we had arrived and no one had scooped it up. Just for fun, I added it to my pile. I got six boxes of items for $40, so I figured that the toaster cost me about $2.

I have heard of toasters selling in the thousand-dollar range, so I am constantly bringing them back to my house. Trust me, most of them don't EVER sell, or they sell very slowly. I think I still have one in my eBay store right now. Why I am still buying kitchen items eludes me. I don't know how to cook, nor do I ever want to learn (despite the cooking lessons my incredibly patient grandmother gave us).

My mom and I put our loot in the minivan and walked over to the toy section to check it out. I saw a cardboard box of video games sitting on the ground and I bent down to take a closer look. The seller wanted $25, which seemed fair, so I pulled out my wad of money and paid her.

Driving away, I checked my pockets to make sure that I still had my dad's $100. It was gone. I started freaking out. We drove back to the sale to ask if anyone had turned it in. I just knew that it had fallen out when I was bending over to examine the box of video games. Nothing.

I got home and was still very upset, but my mood improved a bit when I found that these toasters sell for over $300 at Williams Sonoma when new. Whew! I put it on eBay immediately. The big joke around the office was that my dad would have to take the toaster for repayment instead of his $100. Mo kidded him about it every day. Of course, I paid him back in actual cash.

We couldn't believe it when the toaster ended up selling for almost $200. Mo's final comment to my father was, "You should have taken the toaster."

And, if you can believe my continuing good fortune, three weeks later when I opened the box of video games to list them on eBay, there was my $100 bill!

Afterword

Once again, I am waxing nostalgic now that this writing has come to an end. I experience so many emotions when a book is finally finished: joy, relief, happiness, sadness, and even what could be termed slight depression. The first twenty stories always take the most time. Then from about 21-60, I really get up to speed. Then I breathe a sigh of relief and take my time with 61-80. Around story #81, I put on the brakes. I don't want it to end, so I kind of drag out those last twenty.

Putting the *100 Best* books together involves a much more creative process than most of the books I write. They are fun because they require me not only to write, but also to find ways of weaving in stories about my grandmother, my family and my friends. And then I am always trying to find the perfect side picture. The side picture in #17 has a great story behind it—and I just may tell you about it someday!

It is strange, but most of the time when I sit down and start writing, the story just writes itself, and I don't know where it is taking me until it is finished. More often than not, it has a way of weaving in the side stories and then taking me right back to where I started. It always amazes me when they turn out well. I know that somehow my grandmother has a hand in all this and I still think about her a lot.

If I had one more minute with her, I would tell her how much I love her, what an incredible impact she had on my life and that I still miss her. Now,

I just need to remember to do that with my friends and family that are still here. I find it easy to tell my kids every day (and sometimes every minute) that I love them, but not so easy to tell my parents, siblings and friends. So, to all of you and to those few that I have space to mention—Mom, Dad, Lee, Kiki, Peter, Melanie, Juliette, Maureen—I love you and thank you for being in my life and for helping me with this project!

My brother, Lee, (graphics, photography and layout), my editor, Susan, and my printer, Becky Raney, did such a great job on this book that I want to tell you how grateful I am to have you on my team. You guys rock!

My mom read one of the first drafts and called me to say that I had kept her up all night reading it because she just couldn't put it down! She thought it was awesome! I told her that was because it was all about her family. She laughed and said, "Maybe too much about our family." It is true, I have shared a lot with you in the course of teaching about eBay and I hope it has made the learning experience more enjoyable for you.

Thank you for reading this book and any of the other books I have written. I am honored that you have spent some of your precious time reading my words. I am grateful for all of you and enjoy hearing from you at Lynn@ thequeenofauctions.com. I wish you all the best and God bless.

Order now from The Queen of Auctions:

_____ *The 100 Best Things I've Sold on eBay*—Paperback version—The book that started the series—the original! .... **$15.95 ea**

_____ *i buy*—A 3-ring loose-leaf binder system for tracking your online auction PURCHASES (200 pages w/tab dividers) ...... **$24.95 ea**

_____ *i sell*—A 3-ring loose-leaf binder system for tracking your online auction SALES (200 pages w/tab dividers) .... **$24.95 ea**

_____ "Trash to Cash" Videos-Episodes 1 & 2 on one DVD—This instructional video shows you how to do garage sales and sell on eBay. Watch how $74 turns into $569 in cyberspace on a Saturday morning with Lynn .... **$24.95 ea**

_____ *How to Sell Antiques and Collectibles on eBay...and Make a Fortune!*—This book teaches you the tricks and secrets you need to be successful selling in this very lucrative category........... **$14.95 ea**

_____ *The Unofficial Guide to Making Money on eBay*—Packed with tips and insider information on every aspect of selling on eBay, this book gives pros *and* amateurs an edge. .... **$18.95 ea**

Name_____

Address _____

City _____ State _____ Zip _____

Email _____ Telephone _____

$_____ Items
$_____ Media Mail Shipping ($3 for 1st item and $1 each additional)
$_____ Sales Tax 7.75% CA Residents ONLY

CHECKS Payable to:

$_____ Total Enclosed   All Aboard Inc.
PO Box 14103
Palm Desert, CA 92255

To **CHARGE** your order, please fill in the information below:
_____ American Express _____ Discover _____ Visa _____ Master Card

Account No. _____ Expiration_____

Signature_____

or ORDER ONLINE at www.TheQueenOfAuctions.com or **FAX** (760) 345-9441